#METOO

AND

YOU

EVERYTHING
YOU NEED TO KNOW ABOUT
CONSENT, BOUNDARIES,
AND MORE

HALLEY BONDY

ILLUSTRATED BY
TIMOTHY CORBETT

 ZEST BOOKS
MINNEAPOLIS

To the brave people who shared their stories for this book

Special thanks to content consultant Steve Mandell, educational outreach specialist at Darkness to Light.

Text copyright © 2021 by Halley Bondy

Zest Books™
An imprint of Lerner Publishing Group, Inc.
241 First Avenue North
Minneapolis, MN 55401 USA

For reading levels and more information, look up this title at www.lernerbooks.com.
Visit us at zestbooks.net.

Main body text set in Bembo Std.
Typeface provided by Monotype Typography.

Library of Congress Cataloging-in-Publication Data

Names: Bondy, Halley, 1984- author.
Title: #MeToo and you : everything you need to know about consent, boundaries, and more / Halley Bondy.
Description: Minneapolis : Zest Books, [2020] | Includes bibliographical references and index. | Audience: Ages 11–18. | Audience: Grades 7–9. | Summary: "Author Halley Bondy explores the nuances of emotions, comfort, and discomfort in sexually charged and emotionally abusive situations. Tween readers will learn about consent, harassment, abuse, and healthy boundaries in all types of relationships"— Provided by publisher.
Identifiers: LCCN 2019045943 (print) | LCCN 2019045944 (ebook) | ISBN 9781541581555 (library binding) | ISBN 9781541581593 (paperback) | ISBN 9781728401614 (ebook)
Subjects: LCSH: Sexual consent—Juvenile literature. | Sexual harassment—Juvenile literature. | Sex crimes—Juvenile literature.
Classification: LCC HQ32 .B645 2020 (print) | LCC HQ32 (ebook) | DDC 176/.4—dc23

LC record available at https://lccn.loc.gov/2019045943
LC ebook record available at https://lccn.loc.gov/2019045944

Manufactured in the United States of America
1-47339-47965-6/8/2020

CONTENTS

INTRODUCTION

In 2017 a movement was born.

But first, let's go back for a moment. The phrase "Me Too" was coined in 2006 by an activist named Tarana Burke. Burke used the words *Me Too* to raise awareness about sexual harassment and abuse, particularly in the black community. Burke herself had been abused as a child, and she was finding, to her dismay, that a lot of people around her were saying, "Me too."

However, the phrase and the movement didn't become a household name until 2017, when famous people got involved.

That part began with the powerful movie director Harvey Weinstein.

Weinstein, who produced hits including *Pulp Fiction* and *Shakespeare in Love,* had allegedly been committing all kinds of horrible crimes throughout his entire career. One after another, Hollywood actresses including Alyssa Milano, Salma Hayek, Gwyneth Paltrow, Lupita Nyong'o, Madonna, and more came forward with terrible stories about Weinstein. Ashley Judd said he harmed her career by spreading lies about her because she didn't do what he wanted. After all the allegations came forward, Weinstein was charged for rape, harassment, and other crimes.

The dam had burst. Victims who had felt silenced for so long suddenly felt empowered to speak out about their abusers.

Actor Kevin Spacey, comedian Louis C.K., singer R. Kelly, and news anchor Matt Lauer were among those accused of harassment or far worse.

But the movement didn't end with famous people.

Women, men, cis, trans, and gender-fluid victims everywhere started to speak out about their stories of abuse. The hashtag #MeToo went viral. Survivors were open for the first time about terrible things that had happened to them at school, home, work, among friends, boyfriends, nannies, and more. The movement gave victims the power to speak out, be heard, *and* be believed.

Many of these abuses happened when these victims were your age—middle to high school—but it took growing up into adulthood and feeling empowered by #MeToo to speak out. That shouldn't happen. Children should not live alone with that pain for so long. They shouldn't live with that pain at all. And yet, it did happen. And it still happens a lot.

We still have a long way to go. One in nine girls and one in fifty-eight boys will experience sexual assault by an adult before they turn eighteen. And 40 percent of victims experience abuse at the hands of an older or more powerful child.

Sexual abuse is far too common, and we shouldn't stand for it anymore.

While the internet has made it easier for predators and cyberbullies to do their worst, a majority of abuse still happens at the hands of a trusted family member, friend, teacher, boyfriend, girlfriend, pastor, or acquaintance.

I wish I didn't have to write this book. But I do—for my daughter and for kids everywhere. For the same reason, my husband, Tim, wanted to create the illustrations. Maybe one day, consent, abuse, harassment, retaliation, reporting abuse, counseling, emotional trauma, being an ally, avoiding coercive behaviors, fighting abuse, recognizing abuse, abusive grooming, and staying safe will all be a part of every school's curriculum. Hopefully, one day these things will become crimes of the past.

In the meantime, let this book be your essential guide to #MeToo.

The first chapter is all about the fundamentals of relationships, consent, power dynamics, boundaries, and more. It contains *no* sexual or violent content. Read chapter 1, and then put down the book and decide if you're ready for heavier stuff. If you're not, wait until you are ready, okay?

In the remaining chapters, you'll learn the definitions of abuse. I gathered true stories of abuse from victims and changed all of their names. I also added some fictitious stories to make certain points. You'll know whether a story is true or not. Sometimes, abuse is about relationships and treating other people right, so you'll find stories that have nothing to do with sexual encounters at all.

You'll find out how the events in these stories were handled and how they *should* be handled. You'll learn about seeking justice, seeking emotional help, and what happens when the system fails—which, unfortunately, happens sometimes. You'll learn how to recognize abusive behaviors, and how to avoid committing them yourself. You'll learn the answers to important questions, such as, "How many people lie about being abused?" (short answer: very few), and "Is it abuse if . . . ?" (fill in the blank).

Finally, you will learn how to be an ally to victims and how to fight abuse on a wider scale, from your school to other parts of the globe.

Chapters 2 through 6 contain sexual and violent language for the purpose of instruction. Please read with caution, and don't be afraid to talk to a trusted adult if something in the book is confusing to you.

This book might make you angry or depressed at times. Unfortunately, it's almost impossible to talk about this stuff without shedding a few tears. However, educating yourself about abuse shouldn't keep you from enjoying your life, being happy, and trusting loved ones. Instead, it should motivate you to be part of the change, whether abuse is happening to you, to someone you know, or to someone you *don't* know and whom you'll never meet. It's very possible that you will never encounter any of this stuff in your life—I hope not. Still, everyone should be educated and vigilant if we're going to change the world.

If you're reading this book, you're young, but you are already taking a huge step. You're ready to learn about all this difficult stuff to help make the world a better place. Maybe you're a cis girl, a trans boy, a nonbinary person, or any other identity. This book applies to all of you. If we are going to eradicate abuse, *everyone* needs to be part of the #MeToo movement.

Welcome aboard!

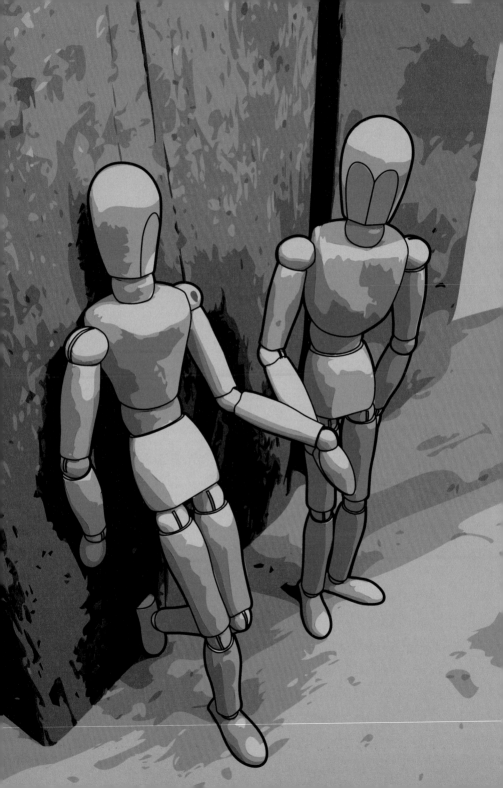

CHAPTER 1

THE BASICS

RELATIONSHIPS, POWER, CONSENT, AND BOUNDARIES

I'm not gonna lie. #MeToo can be a sad and dreary topic. But we're in this together, and the good news is that it all starts with a fun subject you're probably very comfortable with: relationships.

A relationship is any connection you have with someone else. You have a relationship with your mother, your teachers, your friends, the clerk at the grocery store, boyfriends, girlfriends, and even people at school who you don't know very well. Some relationships are more meaningful in your life than others. Every relationship feels different.

You can have a peer relationship, which is a relationship between you and someone who is close to your age. You can be friends, classmates, boyfriend, girlfriend, project partners, and more.

Your relationship with adults or people of very different ages, such as your teachers, parents, mentors, or little sister are *not* peer relationships.

If you're like most kids, relationships just *exist*. Your teachers *happen* to you. Your relatives are just *around*, doing what they do. You get to pick your friends and significant others, but you may not have thought critically about your interactions.

However, in this book, you'll take a step back to examine relationships with a critical eye. What does that mean?

When you're sick, a doctor looks critically at your symptoms. She'll use doctor tools and ask you a bunch of questions until she figures out what's wrong with you. Maybe there's no problem at all, but at least the doctor can confirm that nothing is going on. After all, if there *was* a medical problem, not getting it examined would have made your life worse.

We'll talk about relationships and look critically at them in the same way. Hopefully, all of your relationships are healthy. However, if you don't examine it, an unhealthy relationship can cause a *lot* of damage, kind of like a terrible stomachache that you don't take care of.

The lessons in this chapter will be very handy for recognizing signs of abuse and taking action.

Most of chapter 1 will focus on peer relationships. Chapter 1 has no sexual or violent content. For some of you, this chapter may be all you're prepared to read for now, and that's okay. The lessons in this chapter can be applied to many situations.

For those who *do* feel ready to move on, this chapter serves as a very important stepping-stone into the next chapters, which *do* contain sexual and violent content.

Let's start with the basics: healthy relationships, unhealthy relationships, consent, power dynamics, boundaries, agency, entitlement, and red flags.

HEALTHY RELATIONSHIPS

How healthy are your relationships? A relationship education program for young people called *Power Up, Speak Out!* defines a healthy peer relationship as having the following requirements:

I can be myself.

I can say no.

I have fun.

I treat others well.

Let's dive in. Think about the peer relationships in your life, and consider whether the following statements are true for you.

I can be myself.

That means I don't have to change to be friends with someone.

My peers don't tell me how to dress.

My classmates accept my skin color, my appearance, my sexuality, and my gender identity.

I can hang out with whomever I want to, and my friends still like me.

It's one thing if your peer has different opinions. That's normal, even if it causes arguments from time to time. But if your peer consistently makes you feel bad about who you are, you might be in an unhealthy relationship.

What do you think? Do all of your peer relationships let you be yourself?

I can say no.

It's important to be able to say no if you're uncomfortable or need a change of scene. In a healthy relationship, you must be able to say no without any of the following:

Being put down for it. In a healthy relationship, you can say no without the other person making fun of you. A little light joking happens, but it's another thing if the person really belittles you, makes ruthless fun of you, or talks about it with other people. There is a difference between joking around and cutting someone deeply so that they do whatever another person says.

Pressure. In a healthy relationship, people don't pressure each other. If you say no, the other person should accept it. Again, sometimes people joke around with light pressure, but if someone seriously pressures you and won't let up, this is an unhealthy behavior.

Force. If you are forced to do something, it means that you are left with no choice. If someone forces you to do something you don't want to do, this is a *very* unhealthy behavior.

Fear of scary consequences. If you're afraid to say no because of the consequences, you might be in an unhealthy relationship. For example, a friend in an unhealthy relationship might say that she won't be your friend anymore if you don't do something for her. Or he may threaten to spill your deepest secrets, or he may become so overcome with anger or depression that it's not worth saying no.

Can you say no in all of your peer relationships?

I have fun.

This one is simple. In a healthy relationship, the relationship just *feels* good! You feel like yourself, and there's more fun than drama.

Relationships are never fun *all* the time. But in a peer relationship, the good feelings should generally outweigh the bad.

I treat others well.

You have to hold up your end of the bargain in a healthy relationship too. Here are the ground rules:

Let others be themselves.

Treat others how they want to be treated.

Treat others with respect.

Let others say no.

Have you treated others well? Will you pledge to follow these rules going forward? Awesome. The future is better already.

LIDA & JAY'S STORY (FICTIONAL)

Lida and Jay couldn't wait to see each other between classes in the hall. When Lida sees Jay at his locker, she immediately feels excited.

"Hi, Jay!" she says.

Jay is surprised and beams when he sees her. "Hey there!"

Lida hands him a note, saying, "This note has all the reasons why you should join the theater club with me." She giggles. "You won't be able to argue with any of them."

"Oh yeah?" Jay jokes. "Here's an argument: I can't sing,

dance, or act! I think I'll stick with soccer."

They laugh. Lida is disappointed, but he's probably right. They start to walk down the hall side by side. Jay reaches out and gently touches Lida's hand. Lida reaches back. They're holding hands while walking down the hall.

They approach Lida's friends Robin and Penny. When she sees them, Lida takes her hand away from Jay abruptly. She likes Jay, but she's a little embarrassed and not ready to show public affection yet. They have a quick conversation with Robin and Penny. When they leave, Jay asks: "Are you okay?"

"Yeah," says Lida. She reaches her hand back out to Jay, and they continue walking.

This is an example of a healthy relationship. Here's how we know:

Are they having fun?
Yes. They are both happy when they're around each other.

Can Lida be herself?
Yes. She is allowed to be happy and excited around Jay, and she feels comfortable. She can have her opinions and beliefs about theater without being punished for it.

Can Jay be himself?
Yes. He is allowed to be happy and excited to see Lida, and he feels comfortable. He can have his opinions and beliefs

about theater and soccer without being punished for it.

Can Jay say no?
Yes. He can say no to joining theater without terrible consequences in their relationship. Lida is disappointed, and that's okay, but she respects Jay's opinion.

Can Lida say no?
Yes. Lida can say no to Jay holding her hand when her friends are around. Jay was concerned, but he did not use force or punish Lida for drawing back.

Are they treating others well?
Yes. They are treating each other well because they are following the rules of a healthy relationship.

UNHEALTHY RELATIONSHIPS

Unhealthy relationships break one or more of the rules in the section above—usually a lot of them.

A relationship is unhealthy if these violations happen consistently. An unhealthy relationship often makes you feel uncomfortable or bad.

LIDA & JAY'S STORY, VERSION TWO (FICTIONAL)

Next, let's consider the same basic story but with unhealthy behaviors.

Lida is really angry that Jay hasn't joined theater yet. She storms up to him in the hall and hands him a scathing note at his locker.

"This note has all the reasons why you should join theater," she says. She stuffs the note into his hand.

Jay is totally taken aback. "Look, Lida, I can't. I don't act, I don't sing, I don't dance. I don't want to. I'm a soccer player."

Lida gets very upset and starts to cry. "How could you do this to me?" she says to him. "I thought you cared about me. Obviously, you don't."

Jay doesn't want her to get upset. "Okay, okay. Lida, if it's that important, I'll join theater."

Lida beams with happiness. She grabs Jay's hand, and they start walking down the hall. Jay likes the physical attention, so he keeps holding her hand. In fact, he doesn't want to say it, but it's the only reason why he puts up with Lida. He keeps hoping she'll give him a kiss, or maybe

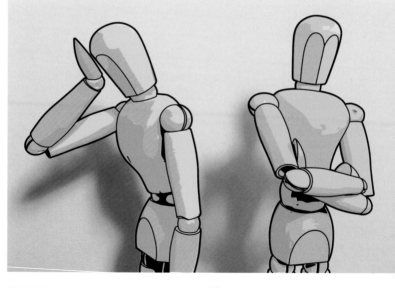

something more.

They run into Lida's friends Robin and Penny. Lida pulls her hand away from Jay while they talk. Jay seethes quietly in anger.

When Robin and Penny leave, Jay says: "Why did you stop holding my hand?"

"Because I don't wanna hold your hand in front of my friends," she said.

Jay storms away. He's annoyed that he agreed to join theater and that she won't even hold his hand. What would he have to do to get a kiss? Or more?

Lida realizes she upset him, so she runs after Jay and grabs his hand. He pulls away, and she pulls his hand back. She apologizes profusely. Finally, Jay gives in and they walk hand in hand again.

Yikes!
This is an unhealthy relationship. How do we know?

Are they having fun?

No. They're stressed, they're upset, and they're fine one minute and angry the next. Lida is very easily upset by Jay's choices. Jay "puts up" with Lida to get physical attention. He doesn't even seem to like being around her. Nobody is having fun.

Can Jay be himself?

No. Jay has to do theater instead of soccer to please Lida.

He changes who he is *just* so that she doesn't get upset.

Can Lida be herself?
No. She doesn't want to hold Jay's hand in front of her friends, but Jay doesn't care how she feels. He only cares about getting physical attention from Lida. To keep Jay interested, Lida doesn't get to be herself, even though she feels embarrassed.

Can Jay say no?
No. Jay can't say no to Lida without her getting upset and threatening to leave him.

Can Lida say no?
No. Lida can't say no to holding Jay's hand without him getting huffy and walking away. She is afraid of losing him, so she doesn't feel like she can say no.

Are they treating others well?
Nope. Lida and Jay are not respecting each other. Each is using the other to get something, and they are not following the rules of a healthy relationship.

So how does an unhealthy relationship happen?
Jay and Lida probably didn't start out this tense. The unhealthy parts of the relationship came slowly. They each want something from the other, but they can't get it. So they act very emotional around each other. They're not looking at the relationship *critically*.

CONSENT

If you give consent, it means that you've said yes, or you have given clear permission. The interaction is *consensual*.

If you do *not* give consent, it means you've said no, or you did *not* give clear permission. The interaction is *nonconsensual*.

Here are *Power Up, Speak Out!*'s direct rules about consent:

- "Consent is an active process between two people."
- "Consent is activity-specific."
- "Consent must be given in a free and clear mindset."
- "Consent can be taken back at any time."

Consent is an active process between two people.

You communicate through words and body language. Consent is when both of you reach an agreement using these skills.

FINN & LUKE'S STORY (FICTIONAL)

Finn and Luke are throwing a ball back and forth. They make eye contact to make sure that the other person is ready to receive the ball. Sometimes, Finn asks, "Are you ready?" when he's not sure if it's okay to throw the ball yet.

This story is consensual. The friends are communicating. They are both consensually playing the game and receiving and throwing the ball using verbal and nonverbal cues.

Next, let's look at a nonconsensual version of this story.

FINN & LUKE'S STORY, VERSION TWO (FICTIONAL)

Finn and Luke are throwing a ball back and forth. Luke tells Finn he needs a time-out to tie his shoes. Finn throws the ball anyway, which catches Luke off guard, and the ball hits him in the side. Luke gets upset and says he doesn't want to play anymore. Finn makes fun of Luke and tries to pressure him into playing more. "Don't be a whiny baby," says Finn.

Finn is throwing the ball *at* Luke, not *with* Luke. They have not communicated or reached an agreement either verbally or nonverbally. Worse, Finn is pressuring Luke and making it very hard for him to say no.

If you say yes to something, you've only said yes to *that particular* activity, and no more than that.

BELLA & TREYA'S STORY (FICTIONAL, INSPIRED BY *POWER UP, SPEAK OUT!*)

Bella and Treya are hanging out in an after-school program. Bella asks to use Treya's phone to call her mom. Treya says sure. Bella calls her mom, but when she's finished, Bella starts flipping through Treya's pictures.

Treya says: "Wait, don't look through my pictures."

"But you said I could use your phone," said Bella. "C'mon. Do you have something to hide? I'll find out."

Bella continues flipping through Treya's pictures, and she shows some of Treya's photos to other kids who are hanging out in the program.

Treya gave Bella consent to use her phone to call her mom. Treya said yes to that particular activity. Treya did not give Bella consent to flip through her photos. This may feel like a violation of Treya's privacy. Treya certainly didn't give Bella consent to show her photos to other people.

Consent must be given in a free and clear mindset.

You can't get consent from someone if they're intoxicated, unconscious, asleep, or not in a sound state.

Also, legally, minors cannot give consent in certain situations with adults (see page 49).

Consent can be taken back at any time.

You can't take back a lot of things. You can't take back mean things you say to people—they already feel hurt. You can't take back the cupcake you gave your friend, because she already ate it.

However, you *can* take back consent. Let's observe the same story but with a twist.

BELLA & TREYA'S STORY, VERSION TWO (FICTIONAL)

Bella asks to use Treya's phone to call her mom. Treya says sure. Bella calls her mom, but when she's finished, Bella starts flipping through Treya's pictures.

Treya says: "Wait, don't look through my pictures."

"But you said I could use your phone," said Bella. "C'mon . . ."

Treya snatches back her phone. "You can't use it anymore."

Treya took the phone back, taking back the consent. It is her phone, and it is her right to do so. Even if Bella **hadn't** broken Treya's boundaries, Treya still has the right to take her phone back at any time. It's her phone, and it's her consent.

POWER DYNAMICS

Every relationship has power dynamics. The question is, Are the power dynamics equal or unequal? If they're unequal, who has *more* power? Who has less?

An equal power dynamic might exist, say, between two close friends of the same age.

An unequal power dynamic might exist between a teacher (who has more power) and a student (who has less) or between a much older student (who has more power) and a younger student (who has less).

Other power dynamics are blurrier. Maybe two peers are the same age, but one student is considered *very* popular and has lots of friends, while the other student is brand new to the school and doesn't have any friends yet. The popular kid has more power in this situation.

In a different dynamic, that *very same kid* with no friends might have more power on the travel soccer team, because he's better at soccer and more liked by the coach, and popularity in school doesn't matter on the field. So, power dynamics can change between peers. However, an adult almost always has more power than a kid. (Sorry. You'll get there.)

If you are lower in the power dynamic, that does not mean you are a worse or weaker person. Everyone has less power sometimes and more power at other times. It can be very hard to control or change power dynamics. You can't turn yourself into a grown-up all of a sudden, for example.

There is a *very* important golden rule in power dynamics. If you take nothing else from this book, take this:

If it's possible and appropriate, the person with more power in a dynamic should use their power

to be good and helpful to those who have less power. Period.

MIA'S STORY (FICTIONAL)

Every February for Black History Month, Mia's history teacher Mrs. Pelham bucks the usual lessons and teaches the class about Martin Luther King Jr., Shirley Chisholm, Angela Davis, and other important civil rights figures. It should be a time of celebration: African Americans have been treated unjustly for centuries, and these heroes defied all odds to fight for equality.

But for Mia, the only African American in her class, it's a very difficult time emotionally.

One February a student named Mike groaned loudly during the discussion.

"Ugh. Why do we have to learn about this?" Mike asked Ms. Pelham. "Mia's the only black person here, and she knows this stuff already. Right, Mia?"

Other students laughed, and some of them agreed with Mike.

Mia slinked deep into her seat, humiliated. She never knew how to respond to attacks like this—and they certainly felt like attacks. Her classmates didn't understand what African Americans have been through, and they had no interest in understanding. This made it feel as though her experience did not matter—and that the other students were hostile to it. Being the only black person in the class, she had no other role models or compatriots to turn to.

Ms. Pelham sternly told Mike and the other laughing students to stay after school. She had a lesson plan prepared to teach them about singling out students and using racial language.

But Ms. Pelham was upset by what she'd witnessed, and she didn't think detention was enough. She noticed that Mia was always especially quiet during these lessons, and that Mia even skipped classes in February, which was *very* unusual for her.

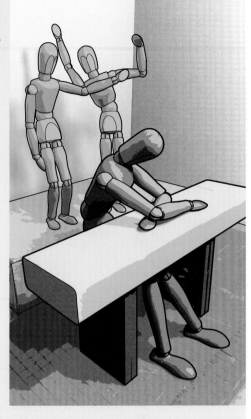

Instead of forcing Mia to speak up about the issue—which could make her feel even *more* singled out—Ms. Pelham held a meeting with the superintendent and the principal. She told them about Mia's situation and brought up ideas to entice more African American students and teachers to join the school, so that students like Mia would feel more at home. She asked the principal if she could create a diversity group for students of color and allies throughout the school, so that students like Mia could find a supportive community.

Ms. Pelham also decided she would incorporate diversity and black history into everyday lessons rather than making it a special day. In the meantime, Ms. Pelham told Mia that she could miss the standard black history class if she felt uncomfortable.

Mia is vastly outnumbered in school. Her skin color makes her different from everyone else in her class. No matter how smart she is, she is low in the power dynamic, especially during discussions of race.

Ms. Pelham and Mia have a teacher-student relationship, so Mia is lower in the power dynamic with Ms. Pelham, as well.

Mike and the rest of Mia's classmates do not acknowledge that they have power over Mia. They don't care or realize that they outnumber her and that African Americans have a traumatic history of being alienated in schools. These students decide (without knowing much about it) that Mia's race isn't a big deal and that they shouldn't have to learn about it. Mike embarrasses Mia in the process, and other kids join in. Mike and Mia's classmates have all broken the golden rule of power dynamics.

Ms. Pelham, thankfully, recognizes her own power in the situation and uses it to make change so that Mia's life at school can be more comfortable. She punishes the students to show everyone that this behavior won't be tolerated. She also hopes that Mike will *learn* something from the punishment. Then she makes an even bigger move by trying to make inclusivity a priority in the school. She's using her power for good. She has followed the golden rule of power dynamics.

If Ms. Pelham had ignored the problem, or worse, if she had *joined* the students in making Mia feel isolated, she would have broken the golden rule of power dynamics.

VULNERABLE/VULNERABILITY

You'll hear the words *vulnerable* and *vulnerability* a lot when talking about power dynamics and abuse. If a person or group is vulnerable, it means that they have less power, and therefore, they are more at risk of being exploited or taken advantage of. People of color, LGBTQ people, people with disabilities, people in poverty, and incarcerated people are vulnerable, as we will discuss throughout the book.

Vulnerability does *not* mean that a person is weak or inferior. That way of thinking is racist, ableist, and toxic. Vulnerability means that a person or group are not the ones in control of their situation and that an abuser can use the opportunity to their advantage. In keeping with the golden rule of power dynamics, less vulnerable people need to stand up for the vulnerable.

BOUNDARIES

Boundaries are all around you. If a pool has a fence around it, that fence serves as a boundary so that nobody accidentally falls in. Some boundaries are harder to see, but they still exist. A good driver doesn't go through red lights, even though he *could*—there's no wall or anything to stop him. But the driver has boundaries. Car safety and stopping at red lights is important to him. Getting in trouble with the law is a boundary he doesn't want to cross.

Breaking some of your own boundaries can be great and healthy. For example, getting out of your comfort zone to join the Spanish club, making friends with someone new, or learning to swim a new stroke even though it scared you in the past are all boundaries worth breaking so that you can grow.

But if someone else disrespects your boundaries, that is *not* okay. In an unhealthy relationship, boundaries are routinely disrespected.

LIZA & ANGIE'S STORY (FICTIONAL)

The funniest thing happened to Liza in science class. After school, she texts her friend Angie about it for twenty minutes straight.

Finally, Angie answers: "Hey, I'm actually studying and turning off my phone. I will turn it back on at 8 and we can talk." Angie turns off her phone.

Liza completely ignores Angie's response and keeps texting her over and over again. When Angie finally turns on her phone, she sees twenty-eight texts from Liza, saying things like "Fine, if you don't wanna answer, we don't have to be friends."

When Angie said she couldn't talk until 8 p.m., she was setting a boundary. Good for her! She knew what she wanted, she spoke out, she was fair, and she was very clear. Liza is perfectly within reason to be disappointed that Angie can't talk. However, she shouldn't disrespect Angie's boundaries. She should have waited until 8 p.m. to text. Instead, Liza took out her disappointment and anger on Angie, and she even tried to manipulate Angie into breaking her personal boundaries. Not okay.

AGENCY

Agency is a type of power. It's a power that *all* of us have. We use our own agency whenever we make our own original choices.

You're using your agency when you start writing or drawing on your own, because it makes you feel good. You're using your own agency to leave a party because you're bored, even though all your friends are telling you to stay. Hopefully, you're using your own agency to take time to read this book and learn about #MeToo. (If your teacher made you, sorry about that.)

In a healthy relationship, you have agency. You choose to hang out with someone. You choose when to text him and when to reply to his messages. You choose to hug him and when to be physical with him. In this healthy relationship, you are using your agency, and he is using his. Maybe sometimes he annoys you or he wants to play *way* more *Fortnite* than you want to play, but you usually speak up when you've had enough. Overall, you both have control in the relationship. It's a beautiful thing.

In an unhealthy relationship, you don't have agency. The other person is making most of the choices: when to hang out, how much to text, what your relationship is called, when to be physical, and what to do with your time together. This person is being selfish and not paying attention to your needs or feelings—your agency does not matter.

You have to learn how to have complete agency. When you were a baby, you had zero agency. Your caregivers had to make every single choice for you. Now, parents may ground you and teachers can make you sit through boring lessons. Sure, this is technically taking away your agency too. But they are doing these things to teach and support you, not to use you for their own selfish ends.

You have agency over many of your relationships, but you don't get to have 100 percent agency over your life until you're an adult. In an ideal world, the adults in your life are helping you get there, unselfishly.

ENTITLEMENT

If a person is entitled to something, that means they deserve it. For example, every child is entitled to a good education and a school environment in which they feel safe.

However, you may also hear the word *entitlement* used in a negative way. For example, older people sometimes say that young people feel entitled to good grades, even though they don't work hard. These people might use phrases like, "There's so much entitlement among kids these days" or "They have such a sense of entitlement." Whether these statements are true or not, entitlement in this case means that a person *thinks* they deserve something, when they actually don't.

In an unhealthy relationship, a person may feel entitled to your time, entitled to your body, entitled to say negative things, or entitled to cross your boundaries. In the story on page 30, Liza felt entitled to Angie's time and attention.

Nobody is entitled to these things. You set the rules, you set the boundaries, and you get to say who is entitled and when.

RED FLAGS

Look out for these *common red flags*, or signs that a relationship may not be healthy:

- The other person actively breaks your boundaries or tries to convince you to break your boundaries.
- Someone much older than you is acting like a peer.
- You don't feel comfortable being alone with this person.
- You don't feel comfortable with the person, period.
- After being with someone, you feel bad about yourself, or they constantly expect you to apologize.
- You feel like you have to be someone else when you're with them.
- This person doesn't care how you feel or tells you that your feelings are wrong.
- Someone tries to turn you against your good friends or family members.
- There is always drama. The person is always upset over something.
- Someone seems nice one minute but not nice the next.

Do you have anyone in your life who raises a red flag? Think about the relationship critically, and decide if the relationship is healthy or unhealthy.

CAN AN UNHEALTHY RELATIONSHIP BECOME HEALTHY?

If you're in an unhealthy relationship, you *might* be able to change it into a healthy one.

Speak up and set boundaries. In the story on page 30, Angie did her best to make her relationship with Liza healthy. She set very clear boundaries and asked Liza only to call her during specific times. If Liza had listened to Angie, perhaps they'd be in a healthy relationship.

Speaking up as Angie did is a great way to try to turn an unhealthy relationship into a healthy one. Sometimes it actually works.

Talk it out. Sometimes talking about a relationship calmly with the other person can help create a healthier dynamic. Meet up in person (it's more personalized than text), and make sure everyone gets to talk about their feelings. Listen. Keep it calm and civil, and keep your goal in mind: you both (hopefully) want a healthier relationship. You're not looking to be right all the time. It may not be solved in the first talk, so try it again!

Arm's length rule. Some people are just good for "arm's length" relationships. Their unhealthy qualities only come out if you get close to them. The best you can do is to keep them at arm's length—not too close, but not completely cut off. This might be the only way to maintain a healthy relationship with a particular person.

Counseling. If you feel you need outside help, counseling is a great option. Guidance counselors can help during conflicts between friends, and sometimes between students and family members. Family counselors are also available to help solve issues in the home.

WHAT IF A RELATIONSHIP *CAN'T* BECOME HEALTHY?

If you don't feel that a relationship can ever be healthy, the best option is to leave the relationship. Sometimes, leaving is an easy option.

For example, if you're in a relationship with a new friend who is starting to show red flags, you can tell them: "I'm sorry, but I don't want to be in a friendship with you. I wish you the best." You don't need to launch into explanations. Do not answer texts or calls. Sometimes this is all you need to drop an unhealthy relationship. Eventually, the other person should move on.

However, sometimes these friends or girlfriends or boyfriends don't let go. They keep luring you back or making your life difficult.

Or maybe the unhealthy relationship is between you and a teacher or you and a family member. It's much harder to drop those relationships and walk away.

If you're in an unhealthy relationship that is hard to leave, do *not* just deal with it. Tell a trusted adult what you're going through. Remember that it is not your fault, and it's much better for you to address an unhealthy relationship than to live with it.

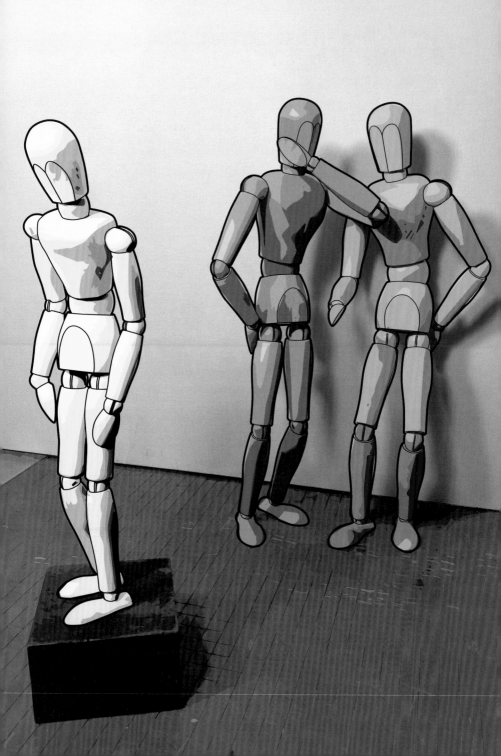

CHAPTER 2

DEFINITIONS
(EXPLICIT)

Content warning: This chapter, and the rest of the book, contain explicit content and definitions of sexual abuse. The content may feel triggering and upsetting, whether you have been abused or not. If you do not wish to read about these difficult terms, stick to chapter 1 until you feel ready.

When we talk about the #MeToo movement, we throw around a lot of terms, such as *harassment*, *abuse*, *consent*, and more. Sometimes these words can get confusing, or they're overused to the point that they lose their meaning.

Hopefully, one day all of this will be taught in schools. Based on the stories I've heard while researching this book, they really should be! But in the meantime, you can read all the definitions in this chapter.

THE BASICS

Me Too The Me Too movement was born in 2006. In 2017 the phrase went viral with a hashtag. People all around the world started to tell their stories of sexual abuse. Celebrities and high-powered executives were suddenly being held account-able for their behavior. (You can read more about this history in this book's introduction.) The purpose of Me Too is to help people feel emboldened to tell their stories, heal, and in some cases, seek justice. You can see the story of the original move-ment's founders' at www.metoomvmt.org.

Abuse Abuse comes in many, many forms. It can refer to any type of purposeful, malicious wrongdoing against another per-son. Abuse includes harassment, coercion, rape, molestation, assault, retaliation, and even bullying. Abuse can be sexual, ver-bal (using words), emotional, physical, or any combination of these. It can range from unwanted touching to violence, from name-calling online to humiliating someone about their body, or it could mean manipulating a friend into doing something they don't want to do.

Victim A person who is being abused.

Abuser A perpetrator. One who abuses.

Predator One who engages in predatory behavior. This is a person who very purposefully tries to make sexual or romantic contact with a victim to abuse or control. Asking someone on a date is *not* predatory behavior. Telling someone they're pretty with the hope that maybe they'll go out with you is *not* predatory behavior.

Asking someone on a date after they've repeatedly said no, showing up at their doorstep, trying to touch them, threatening them, and pressuring them to send you photos—all of these actions are predatory.

MELODY & FRANKIE (BASED ON A TRUE STORY)

Melody, a middle school student, was blind. She worked with tutors and paraprofessionals who escorted her around school and provided private lessons. Frankie was an adult tutor assigned to help Melody with algebra. He was not disabled.

He'd been working with Melody for a few months. Melody and her family trusted and liked Frankie, and she was doing very well in math.

One day, as usual, Melody and Frankie were alone in an empty officelike room. Melody was working on a math problem when, suddenly, she felt Frankie's hands on her. He grabbed her breasts and her crotch. Melody froze, terrified. Eventually, he let go, and he simply continued the lesson as if nothing had happened. When he sensed that Melody was upset, he said, "I think we both got a little carried away."

Melody didn't even feel connected to her body in that moment. She felt as though she was somewhere else.

Afterward, Melody felt incredibly vulnerable. Here was this guy who had full access to her. She'd always been a hands-on and affectionate person, but now she felt like she couldn't trust anyone. Melody felt that she could be attacked by anyone she trusted and that they could just run away undetected.

This very upsetting story is an example of the vulnerability of certain populations. Students with disabilities are usually isolated from their peers, and they spend a lot of time with adults. Those factors make them vulnerable to abuse. Frankie violated the golden rule of power dynamics in the worst way. He is an abuser. Melody probably needs counseling to handle this terrible incident, and Frankie, an adult, must be prosecuted.

Pedophile An adult who is sexually attracted to kids. Any adult who engages with a child sexually is committing a crime, including pedophiles who look at child pornography. The child is a victim and is not committing any crime.

Human Trafficking Human trafficking is when abusers treat people as if they're items to be bought and sold. In some cases, abusers are looking to create explicit photos to sell. In worse cases, they are looking for human beings to kidnap and exploit.

Traffickers are often found online prowling for children by pretending they're either other children or celebrities.

BIEBER FAN'S STORY (TRUE)

In 2017 a nine-year-old girl was browsing through Justin Bieber's Instagram page. Suddenly, she received a private message from another user. This user told her that he knew Bieber and that he would arrange a text message connection between them if she followed his instructions. First, she had to join the social media app Kik (which had more anonymous features than Instagram). There, she started receiving messages from somebody claiming to be Justin Bieber. This person told her to send him nude photos and videos of herself and threatened to harm her if she didn't.

The girl obliged. Then she deleted the messages. She told no one.

Two years later, this person resurfaced and demanded new photos and videos. This time, the girl told her mom, who told the police.

"Justin Bieber" turned out to be a twenty-four-year-old man from Massachusetts with no connections to the real Bieber. The man had been committing similar crimes against other girls across the country.

Trafficking is extremely scary and illegal, but you can protect yourself by remembering these simple rules:

Never, ever agree to meet with a stranger you met online, even if the stranger sounds cool and friendly, or if someone sounds like a celebrity or another kid. Remember, the stranger could be really skilled at lying.

Never tell a stranger where you live or where you go to school.

Never, ever send nude photos of yourself to anyone, _especially_ not to strangers on the internet, no matter what they say.

Be wary of grooming behaviors (see page 55).

Never get into a vehicle alone with someone without your parents' or caregiver's knowledge.

If you think you've encountered a trafficker, tell a trusted adult immediately and do not engage with the suspected trafficker ever again.

TYPES OF ABUSE

Inappropriate Behavior, Improper Touch These descriptions are used in "lighter" incidents of abuse, such as when a person makes strange sexual comments or touches someone in a way that feels creepy or uncomfortable, intentional or not.

Even if an incident is not all-out assault or if it feels like it's no big deal, it still needs to be acknowledged and dealt with, especially if it's making someone uncomfortable.

GIANNA & MR. DENSCH'S STORY (TRUE)

Everybody loved Gianna's teacher, Mr. Densch. He was really funny and cool. But lately, he'd been acting strangely. All of a sudden, he wouldn't let anybody use the bathroom during his class. The class was two hours long! This meant that in addition to forcing kids to hold their bladders, girls couldn't change their tampons when they had their periods.

One of Gianna's classmates complained to Mr. Densch in private about the menstruation issue. After that, every time a girl asked to go to the bathroom, Mr. Densch would say to the entire class: "Oh, I guess I have to let you, because you're on your period!" The other kids, especially the boys, would giggle.

Mr. Densch started to do other stuff too. One time, he grabbed a girl's arm when she was trying to walk away from his desk after a lesson. She told him to let go, yet he held on for one second longer before letting her go. The tone

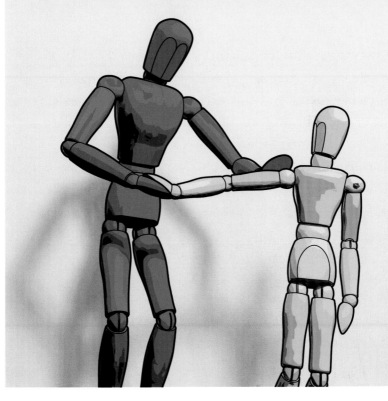

was jokey. Nobody was hurt. Everybody moved on.

He would get kinda close to students' faces when he was going over their papers at their desks . . . but maybe Gianna was just reading too much into it.

Gianna felt uncomfortable and embarrassed by all of this, and she was starting to feel weirded out around Mr. Densch. It sucked, because he'd been her favorite teacher. He was such a cool guy, and everyone in the class loved him. And none of these things were a big deal on their own. It's not as if he were attacking anyone. And yet, Gianna continued to feel weird going into his class. Weirder and weirder each day.

When it comes to not letting kids go to the bathroom, well, there's likely a school policy against that. Everything else could fall under inappropriate behavior or improper touch. It's possible that Mr. Densch doesn't know that his behavior is affecting students or making them uncomfortable. It's also possible that he **does** know. It really doesn't matter. The behavior is inappropriate, and it's creating an uncomfortable environment for students, which is not okay.

Unfortunately, on top of making Gianna feel weird, Mr. Densch has put her in a tight spot. She doesn't know whether to report him, since these incidents seem small and since he's so beloved in the school. This story continues on page 116 in the chapter on reporting.

Sexual Harassment A kind of sexual abuse in which an abuser harasses a victim. The abuser purposely annoys, intimidates, or threatens the victim using sexual language, gestures, or ideas. Sometimes harassment can be irritating. Other times, it can make a victim feel unsafe. It is always wrong.

GRETA'S, NICO'S, AND NOAH'S STORIES (TRUE STORIES WITH DETAILS CHANGED)

One day, Greta was changing her maxi pad in the school bathroom. Tina happened to overhear her. Afterward, every time Tina passed Greta in the hallway, she yelled, "Greta, don't bleed on me!" Everyone around her laughed. Greta also laughed to seem okay with it, but really, she was embarrassed and upset and wished that Tina would stop.

Every day, Sean asked Nico to send him nude pics of her from her phone. She laughed it off, but she felt weird about it. Sean kept asking. Then one day, Sean's friend Paulo said to Nico, "I heard you sent Sean some nudes." Sean had been lying! Nico felt scared. Were there nudes of her out there somehow? How many people believed this rumor?

Noah was walking to class when he saw a piece of paper taped to a hallway wall. The piece of paper said "Best Butt" and "Worst Butt," with a bunch of kids' names written down. He was listed under Worst Butt. He felt humiliated. How long had this been posted?

Tina, Sean, and the mysterious butt ranker—these are all perpetrators who probably just think what they're doing is a funny joke. It's actually sexual harassment, and their actions could frighten or traumatize someone. Greta, Nico, and Noah might feel that they have to play along and think it's funny, but they don't. Unless they're **really** in on the joke (which they aren't), they are victims.

Slut-Shaming Slut-shaming can be a form of sexual abuse or sexual bullying. Slut-shaming is when a person or group gangs up on someone—usually a girl—and bullies her about her sexuality. A *slut* is supposedly promiscuous, but the term is often used merely to shame someone.

Slut-shaming is a way to put someone down and to exert control and power over her. It does not mean that the victim is actually promiscuous (and if she is, how is that any of your business?). *Slut* is a completely meaningless word used to keep girls down. Once in a while, a girl might enjoy owning the title, but that's different from sexual bullying.

It does not matter if a girl actually engaged in sexual behavior or not. Bullying is never okay, and neither is slut-shaming.

LEIDY & NADIA'S STORY (TRUE)

Leidy was new to her middle school, and she was eager to make friends. Nadia, who was already very popular, immediately felt threatened by Leidy. So Nadia started telling her male friends that Leidy was a total slut.

Nadia asked Leidy for her phone number. Leidy, thinking that Nadia wanted to be her friend, gave it to her.

Nadia then spread Leidy's phone number among all the boys. She told them that Leidy would do *anything* they wanted. She repeated over and over that Leidy was a "gross slut." She texted Leidy: "I heard that you hooked up with like twelve guys last year."

Leidy was confused, and wrote "What? No." But Nadia had already texted everyone the story. Every day, Leidy received notes from anonymous sources calling her a slut.

One day, Mikel—one of Nadia's friends—started texting Leidy and flattering her. Leidy was happy to have some positive attention. Eventually, Mikel convinced Leidy to send him a suggestive photo of her.

Mikel texted the photo to all of his friends, including Nadia. And if it was even possible, the bullying got worse after that.

There's no doubt about it that Nadia and Mikel are bullying and that all the other students are being complicit, or helping, in the bullying. They are slut-shaming Leidy. Even if Leidy **had** hooked up with twelve guys the previous year, nobody has the right to bully someone. The word *slut* is a meaningless insult here. It is only a tool to keep Leidy down. These students are doing everything they can get away with, and they are doing terrible emotional damage to Leidy.

It should also be noted that technically, photos of a naked child are considered child pornography and are illegal, even if they are passed around among peers. Unfortunately, this law isn't often legally enforced unless an adult is involved in seeking out the photos. However, these photos are still illegal, and many advocates are fighting for child nudes to be a crime, no matter who asked for them.

Abuse of Power A person who has more power in a power dynamic should never use this power for selfish, cruel, or illegal means. If they do, it's called an abuse of power. We will be discussing many examples of this throughout the book.

Peer Abuse About 40 percent of sexual abuse victims were abused by an older or more powerful child. This is called peer abuse, whether it's a family member or a class-mate. Peer abuse can be tough to recognize and, unfor-tunately, even tougher to punish. Sometimes it can be hard to tell the difference between a peer being abusive or just curious.

Besides the list of abusive behaviors listed throughout this section, the anti–sex abuse organization Stop It Now! created a handy guide that outlines appropriate versus inappropriate behavior by age. See pages 50 and 51.

Rape Rape refers to forced oral or penetrative intercourse. The victim does not consent to sex. It is also considered rape if the victim is unconscious, incapacitated, intellectually disabled, or a minor, because any of those people cannot consent to sex.

Here are a few other terms about rape that you might hear:

Date rape or acquaintance rape: These phrases are sometimes used to describe rape between two people who know each other. They could be people who are friends, neighbors, dating, or any other kind of relationship. This does not make the crime any lighter or better. In eight out of ten rape cases, the victim knows the rapist.

Stranger rape: A "stranger rape" is when the rapist and victim do not know each other. This might occur as an attack in a public space, as a home invasion, or if a stranger tries to gain the victim's trust by luring them into a car, by encouraging them to drink too much alcohol, or by other means.

Statutory rape: Generally, when a person over eighteen has sex with a person below the "age of consent," this is called statutory rape, *even if* the younger person consented. Legally, the rules and the age of consent are different in each state, but the age usually ranges from sixteen to eighteen.

Sexual Assault Sexual assault can refer to rape, molestation, unwanted sexual touching, or forcing someone into a sexual act. Sexual assault is violence, and it is illegal.

Molestation Typically, molestation refers to all illegal sexual touching. Molestation might include taking pornographic photos, fondling somebody's genitals against their will, or any "indecent act" between an adult and a child.

APPROPRIATE AND INAPPROPRIATE BEHAVIOR BY AGE

	Common Behavior	Uncommon Behavior
Preschool Age (0–5)	• Will have questions and express knowledge relating to: - differences in gender and private body parts - hygiene and toileting - pregnancy and birth • Will explore genitals and can experience pleasure • Showing and looking at private body parts	• Having knowledge of specific sexual acts or explicit sexual language • Engaging in adultlike sexual contact with other children
School Age (6–8)	• Will need knowledge and have questions about - physical development, relationships, and sexual behavior - menstruation and pregnancy - personal values • Experiment with same-age and same-gender children, often during games or role-playing. • Self-stimulation in private is expected to continue.	• Adultlike sexual interactions • Having knowledge of specific sexual acts • Behaving sexually in a public place or through the use of phone or internet technology.
School Age (9–12) Hormonal changes and external influences, such as peers, media, and internet, will increase sexual awareness, feelings, and interest at the onset of puberty.	• Will need knowledge and have questions about - sexual materials and information - relationships and sexual behavior - using sexual words and discussing sexual acts and personal values, particularly with peers • Increased experimentation with sexual behaviors and romantic relationships. • Self-stimulation in private is expected to continue.	• Regularly occurring adultlike sexual behavior. • Behaving sexually in a public place.

Common Behavior	Uncommon Behavior
Adolescence (13–16) • Will need information and have questions about - decision-making - social relationships and sexual customs - personal values and consequences of sexual behavior • Self-stimulation in private is expected to continue. • Girls will begin menstruation; boys will begin to produce sperm. • Sexual experimentation between adolescents of the same age and gender is common. • Voyeuristic behaviors are common in this age group. • Sexual intercourse will occur for approximately one-third of teens.	• Masturbation in a public place. • Sexual interest directed toward much younger children.

Source: Stop It Now!

Molestation can occur between peers, but it usually refers to incidents between an adult and child or a much older child and a younger child.

Stalking Stalking is like harassment, only it tends to include more menacing behavior, such as repeatedly following, watching, or contacting a victim without consent. Stalking might involve technology, such as the perpetrator constantly emailing, using GPS to track, or installing video cameras to watch a victim.

Incest Incest is an inappropriate sexual relationship between family members, such as a father and a daughter, an aunt and a nephew, two brothers, and so on. Incest laws vary by state, but most states illegalize sexual relations between close family members. Of course, any adult who attacks a child is committing a crime, no matter the relation. If a victim is within the close family, the attacker is committing the crime of incest as well as assault or rape, depending on the nature of the crime.

Sodomy/Sodomize These words are sometimes used to describe the act of forcibly penetrating a victim in his or her anus. *Rape* and *anal penetration* are other words for sodomy.

ABUSIVE BEHAVIORS TO WATCH OUT FOR

Coercion Coercion is the act of pushing a person into doing something that they don't want to do. Coercion can be physical, but people usually use the word for coercive language, blackmail, and threats. Coercion does not have to be sexual.

COERCION STORIES
(FICTIONAL)

Marlene tells Jackie that she won't invite her to her family's big New Year's Eve party that year unless Jackie gives Marlene her expensive, amazing shoes.

Coach K tells one of the middle-grade soccer players, Mick, that she won't let Mick play midfield this year unless she kisses her.

Rick, who is eighteen, has been inviting Glen over to play video games for weeks. Glen is thirteen. Things start to get creepy when Rick says Glen isn't allowed to tell his parents about their friendship. Rick says that if Glen tells his parents, they will both be arrested and Glen will never see his parents again.

Jax invited Amy to a party. She was excited to go, but as it turned out, she was the only girl there. Jax and his friends told Amy to play a game by making out with all of them. Amy felt weird and said no. Jax said he would tell everyone in school that she did *way* more than make out with them if she didn't do it. Amy realized that the boys were surrounding her, and she felt threatened.

Whether it's lies, threats, or blackmail, these people are asserting their power to make other people do things they don't want to do. The victims feel powerless and obligated to obey. This is coercion. Amy's incident has begun with coercion, and it seems as if it may end in assault.

Manipulation Manipulation is when a perpetrator tries to control or influence a victim, usually without the victim even realizing it. Coercion is a type of manipulation, but coercion tends to be negative and very in your face. Manipulation *can* be negative, but sometimes it can feel so positive that people don't even know they're being manipulated.

MR. FLINT & BRIGITTE'S STORY (FICTIONAL)

Mr. Flint constantly tells Brigitte that she's the smartest girl in the school and that nobody understands her. He tells her that *he alone* recognizes her talent. He says it all the time in private, and he frequently invites her to stay after school to work on special projects with him. He says he will wait for her to come to him. Brigitte is shy and doesn't hear things like this very often, so she's flattered. She wants Mr. Flint to keep liking her and approving of her.

Okay. Let's take a deep breath. It's possible that Mr. Flint is being honest and that he really **does** want Brigitte to succeed. Let's hope! However, he seems to be alone with her a lot, and he's pushing for even **more** private time. Either Brigitte really **is** that special, or he's using a common abusers' tactic of singling out kids who don't have much confidence and making them feel really special.

If Mr. Flint **is** an abuser, he has manipulated Brigitte. She craves his compliments and his attention. He might take advantage of her when they are alone. This is also an abuse of power, since, as Brigitte's teacher, he has power over her life.

Perhaps Brigitte should grill him for details about the projects and tell her parents about the interactions they've been having. She could insist to Mr. Flint that she bring a few friends, or she might even tell a school official that she plans to stay with Mr. Flint after school. If Mr. Flint is being honest, he will be **very** open to all of these precautions.

If he continues to insist on getting Brigitte alone, that is a **serious** red flag. There is **no** reason why he needs to be alone with Brigitte for her academic success.

We can hope he is not an abuser, but manipulation can start small, and if something feels weird, it's good to stay vigilant.

Escalating Escalating is when an abuser's behavior starts with small behaviors (see the previous example of Brigitte and Mr. Flint) but grows more intense over time. An abuser may escalate his or her behavior, perhaps from harassment to all-out assault. This does not happen every time, but it can happen, especially when an abuser is *grooming* a victim (see below).

Grooming Grooming is scary business. It refers to the slow and steady manipulation of a victim until she (or he) is completely under the abuser's control. Sometimes, people are groomed into things like prostitution or trafficking. Other times, they are groomed so the abuser can abuse the victim over a long period.

Step 1: Flattery and Cockiness All of a sudden, Gina's much older schoolmate Harrison starts paying a lot of flattering attention to her. He gives her tons of compliments and gifts that she never expected. It feels as though the relationship is getting extremely serious very fast. Harrison is leading the charge on everything. He tells her great stories about himself, such as how rich his family is and what an important musician

he is. He tells Gina he knows Taylor Swift's songwriter and will introduce her someday. Gina thinks he's really cool, and since he's a couple of years older, he has more life experience than she has.

Here, an abuser is making a victim feel extremely special without giving her a lot of time or space to question things. He is almost overwhelming her with attention. Gina enjoys and will begin to crave his love and affection. It feels like love, but if she's dealing with an abuser, it's not. Also, abusers sometimes lie about themselves or embellish facts.

Step 2: Breaking Boundaries Harrison asks Gina to do things she's not comfortable with, including skipping class to hang out with him. He calls her very late at night, which is kinda cool, but it also makes Gina tired during the day. He starts to talk about pornography and how much he wants to watch it with her. He says that he loves her so much and that it would bring them closer. Gina feels nervous about it, but she loves him, so she goes with it. Watching porn is not that bad, really.

Harrison is starting small with watching porn, so it doesn't feel bad. But nothing is okay if Gina is not comfortable. Her gut is correct. If something feels wrong, it is. However, an abuser can be *really* good at convincing a victim that her gut is wrong.

Step 3. Keeping Secrets Harrison instructs Gina not to tell anyone about the pornography. Since he is a few years older than her, he says that nobody should know about their relationship at *all*. He starts saying things like, "If people find out, we'll both get in trouble, and you'll never see me again" and "What we have is special, and everyone else will try to destroy it."

Out of fear, victims of grooming sometimes keep these secrets for years, decades, or even their whole lives.

Step 4. Isolation from Friends and Family Harrison says negative things about Gina's friends and parents. Gina loves and trusts her friends and parents, but they do get on her nerves sometimes. For example, Gina once told Harrison that her mom can be very controlling, so Harrison keeps telling her things like, "Your mom is trying to control you. You should be free. You're too smart and beautiful." Gina starts to feel as if he might be right.

Over time, Harrison is trying to convince Gina that these people are bad and that she needs to get away from them. However, these people *aren't* bad, even if Gina has normal disagreements with them sometimes. Harrison is using manipulation to try to isolate Gina so that he has more control over her.

He doesn't want anyone else in her life influencing her.

Step 5: Brainwashing Harrison has made Gina feel that he's the most important person in her life. Everything has become about him. They call and text constantly. Gina wonders how he is going to be feeling each day and how she will dress and act to make him happy. She hopes he'll be in a good mood. He gets jealous of her male friends, so she no longer speaks to them. Harrison thinks school is stupid, so Gina starts to act up in class and let her grades slip too. He tells her he's going to be a famous musician, and she believes him. Everyone in her life thinks Harrison is awful and a total liar, but Gina feels as though she and Harrison have a higher love—too high for anyone to understand. (Guess who fed those words to her?) She doesn't tell anyone about the bad stuff—such as how she's not getting enough sleep because Harrison insists on all-night phone calls. When people ask her why she looks so tired these days, she says she ate something funny.

She's in so deep that she doesn't even let *herself* feel the bad stuff.

Gina is being brainwashed, which means that she is adopting Harrison's way of thinking, and it controls her. At this point, she cannot see how wrong and tragic this is. She can only see how great he is and how much Harrison has saved her from a boring existence.

Step 6: Escalating Requests, Sexual and Otherwise Harrison begins to ask Gina for new things. He insists that they start taking pornographic photos of themselves to sell on the internet and that they drop out of school together. These things seem crazy, and yet he makes them sound so reasonable.

Harrison knows that Gina will do anything he wants

her to do. She probably would have said no if Harrison had suggested these things in the beginning of their relationship, but he has whittled her down. Harrison might be doing this all on his own, but given the nature of his requests, it might be that Harrison is working with people on the internet who sell sexual photos of minors and that the whole relationship is a lie. This sounds wild, but it happens. No matter what the other circumstances are, this relationship has gotten abusive and untenable for Gina.

Step 7: Escalating Violence and Abuse Harrison forces Gina to make out with him. He pushes her into his car when she says she has to go to class. He tells her that he does these things because he loves her. He also says he will be completely lost without her. Then he tells Gina that she's fat and that nobody else will love her the way he does. She believes everything he says.

Harrison maintains control over Gina by using abuse and terror. He wants to keep her dependent on and afraid of him and to decrease her confidence. If she feels confident or independent, she may leave him.

Step 8: Periods of Kindness Sometimes Harrison is kind and loving. After a day of abuse, he becomes super apologetic toward Gina. He gives her gifts and acts loving, generous, and fun. For a moment, Gina feels as if the relationship is good, as it was in the beginning. What was she even worried about?

Abusers often go back and forth like this. Harrison is trying to confuse Gina so that she feels safe and comfortable again, without any time or space to question the abuse. At this point, he has also alienated her from family and friends, so she has nobody to talk to about her concerns.

Even though her family keeps pressing her to talk about it, she feels embarrassed or she feels that he will be mad at her if she speaks up.

Step 9: Coercive Threats Sometimes when Gina tries to leave the relationship, Harrison goes on the offensive. He threatens to blackmail her with photos he's taken of her, saying he'll post them everywhere online. He says that if she leaves, they'll both go to jail and that he'll kill himself from the agony of losing her. She believes him or she feels guilty or both, so she stays. She hopes that he'll be nice to her again soon and that they'll be happy again.

Like the periods of kindness, these threats are mostly lies. In these moments, Harrison is desperate, saying anything he can to get her to stay. He likes having control over Gina. Perhaps he truly loves her and thinks this is the only way to get someone to love him back. Perhaps he just wants to sell pictures of her. His reasoning does not matter as far as Gina—and her life—are concerned.

Step 10: Total Control Gina is trapped in Harrison's abusive cycle until she can break free. She sees that he is not going to be a professional musician—he never practices and doesn't really know Taylor Swift's songwriter—but it doesn't seem to matter anymore. She is ashamed of how dark her life has gotten. The only person she can talk to is Harrison. To Gina, there is no way out, so she might as well stay. After all, Harrison is the only one who will love her.

It will take support, separation from Harrison, psychiatric counseling, and legal interventions to help Gina break free. In the world, Harrison is not particularly important. He is clearly a person who needs mental health care. But to Gina, he has become the source of her joy, her sadness, her future plans, her mental health, and her sexuality. She has let herself disappear under his control.

It's important to note that some of these actions alone aren't sure signs of grooming. Sometimes healthy relationships become serious quickly, sometimes regular people say mean things about your loved ones, and sometimes you need to keep your relationship a secret for legitimate reasons. These things alone do not always indicate grooming, but together, they form an abusive pattern. It sounds like fiction, but unfortunately, it happens all the time.

Grooming can be within a peer-to-peer relationship, like the one between Harrison and Gina. It can happen between a more powerful person and a less powerful peer. It can happen between an adult and a child. It can happen between a trafficker and a trafficking victim. It can happen online or in real life.

Grooming can also take place within a family, which means that the victim has potentially been groomed for his or her entire life. For example, if a stepfather wants to molest his stepdaughter whenever he wants for years and years, he might groom her into believing that this is okay, and normal, and teach her not to tell anyone.

AFTERMATH

Reporting Reporting refers to when victims tell an authority figure about abuse they have suffered. They may choose to report an incident to a school guidance counselor, a parent, a teacher, a police officer, a doctor, a therapist, or someone else.

Once reported, many of these authority figures have to take action by telling certain other authority figures. This is called mandatory reporting. For instance, a therapist may be legally required to report abuse to the local department of child protective services.

Many victims do not report abuse because they fear retaliation (see page 63) or because they don't trust authority figures to stop the abuse. For more on reporting and mandatory reporting, turn to chapter 4.

Civil Rights If you are abused, your civil rights are being violated.

Title IX is a federal law that prohibits various forms of sex discrimination, including sexual harassment, gender-based bullying, and sexual violence, in schools that receive federal funding. Therefore, your school must do everything in its power to either prevent sexual abuse or to handle it properly if it occurs. It is your right as a student in the United States.

If your civil rights have been abused, you can file a civil case against the school, the abuser, or other people involved. Usually the victim asks for damages such as money or other compensation.

Criminal Cases You may also be the victim of a crime, which is closer to what you've probably seen on TV. After a crime, the law gets involved and an abuser might face fines or jail time. Crime victims have rights, including the right to be protected from the accused, the right to be informed of any court proceedings, and the right to privacy and dignity.

The US Department of Justice lists all crime victims' rights on its website: https://www.justice.gov/usao/resources/crime-victims-rights-ombudsman/victims-rights-act.

Read more about victims' legal rights in chapter 4.

Retaliation Retaliation basically means revenge. Abusers sometimes use retaliation against their victims or threaten to use it to keep them quiet about the abuse. Retaliation scares victims, and it's a major reason why many victims do not report their abuse.

JOHAN & KERRY'S STORY (FICTIONAL)

Johan tells Kerry that he's gay. It's a huge relief to tell someone, and he thinks that Kerry is a trustworthy friend.

Later, during an algebra test, Kerry peeks at Johan's answers and copies them down to the number. Johan is a bit upset—he'd studied hard—but Kerry is a good friend and he wants to help her out.

While grading the tests, their algebra teacher notices that Kerry and Johan gave the exact same answers and notes. He tells Kerry and Johan that they'll both have to stay after school until one of them admits they cheated.

Johan hopes that Kerry will come clean. But instead, she says to him privately, "If you tell on me, I'll tell your parents that you're gay. You have to take the fall."

Johan is stunned. His parents are very conservative, and his whole world would be devastated if they found out.

Johan feels hurt and betrayed, but he decides it would be easier to just take the blame.

Kerry is using *retaliatory* threats against Johan. If he doesn't shut up and follow her orders, she will unleash his worst nightmare. Because of these threats, Johan is forced to take the blame for something he didn't do, and Kerry gets off scot-free.

Would Kerry have told Johan's parents, or is it just an empty threat? Who knows? But she used this very vulnerable point in Johan's life as a power move. She is abusing her power as a friend who knows Johan's deepest secret.

Sexual abusers often keep their victims in line by using similar retaliatory tactics.

Trauma Trauma is the natural emotional response that victims feel after being sexually abused. When people are traumatized, their brains change. Until they deal with the trauma in a productive way, such as through counseling, their brains are forever changed, and they will have trouble dealing with regular life.

Trauma can crop up in different ways. Right after abuse happens, a victim might bury feelings of terror. But later, the same victim may have difficulty sleeping, eating, or getting into healthy relationships. Victims of abuse may start using drugs or alcohol to medicate their pain. They might start cutting themselves or do other self-harm. Or they might seem extremely happy all the time to hide what happened. One study found that 33 percent of rape victims contemplate suicide and 13 percent attempt it. Sometimes they don't even know that sexual abuse is why they're struggling.

For kids, trauma can hit particularly hard because their brains are still developing. Living through trauma as a child can cause severe anxiety, memory problems, inability to concentrate, and difficulty learning. Their trauma will follow them into adulthood. Often victims blame themselves for what happened because it is easier to believe than to face the painful truth.

Unfortunately, trauma does not just go away or wear off. It can last a whole lifetime, and drugs, booze, or any other escape can't get rid of it. Only proper treatment and support can help a person acknowledge their trauma and heal. Then a victim can help others.

Imagine that you're swimming forward while holding a beach ball underwater. The beach ball wants to pop up above the water, but you don't want to let it. You don't want the other swimmers to know that you're carrying this beach ball around. So you swim with the beach ball as best as you can, even though it messes with your swimming technique. Sometimes you can't use your arms or your legs. But whatever it takes to keep that ball underwater, you'll do it. You get so used to the beach ball that you forget it's there.

The beach ball is like trauma. You can bury it and even forget it, but it will still negatively affect your life and functioning. Counseling can help you take the ball out from under you slowly, in a healthy way, so that it doesn't just pop up and give you a terrible shock. It's almost impossible to do this alone, and hurting yourself never helps.

KAYE'S STORY (TRUE, VERY DISTURBING)

When Kaye was eleven years old, her sister's twenty-six-year-old friend Jack started coming around to the house. Over and over, he would knock on the front door and ask Kaye if her older sister was home. Over and over, she would tell him that her sister was away. She thought Jack was just a forgetful guy. Still, Jack would stay and chat Kaye up and tell her that she was pretty. She was flattered.

One day, he asked if her parents were home. They were not. They were away on a trip. A nanny was inside, but she was mostly occupied with Kaye's younger sister. Jack offered Kaye a ride on his moped. She agreed. His moped was cool.

They rode on the moped for quite some time. Much longer than Kaye expected. Jack took Kaye to the woods. There he stopped and offered her a beer. She took a sip. Her drink was likely drugged, because she felt hazy after that.

Jack raped her in the woods. He then brought her to his home, where he raped her repeatedly. He brought over a friend who also raped her. He had to go to work at one point, so he handcuffed her so she couldn't leave. She was held captive for three days, in two locations.

Jack put Kaye in his car to take her somewhere. Kaye was pretty out of it from dehydration, lack of food, and being drugged, but she recognized something on the highway. She realized that she was fairly close to her house and that if she didn't act now, she might never go home.

She pulled the emergency brake, then spun the steering wheel, sending the car into a tailspin. She opened the passenger door and ran out, deep into the woods. She buried herself under leaves and heard Jack walking around, calling for her. He did not find her.

She stayed under the leaves, petrified, for the rest of the day. Eventually, Kaye found the courage to emerge. She walked home.

She told the nanny that she'd been at a friend's house. The nanny believed her and didn't want to make any trouble with her parents, who were still on a trip. Kaye went right to bed.

She believed it was her fault. She had trusted Jack. She had agreed to ride his moped. She had kissed boys before this, and she had had sexual thoughts. To her, this was all her fault. So she told no one. Jack tried to reach out to Kaye and tell her that he was sorry and that he loved her and that she was his girlfriend. She trusted her gut to stay away from him.

The next year in school, Kaye started cutting her skin with razor blades to harm herself. She started yelling at her parents for no reason. She developed a disorder called trichotillomania in which she compulsively pulled out her hair. She developed anxiety and depression.

Eleven years later, Kaye was able to get help and tell some people what had happened. She is now an adult in her thirties, and she still feels triggered by certain things, which means that she feels traumatic sensations when exposed to certain stimulus, including true crime television. She believes that Jack has hurt other children, which hurts her every day.

In this devastating story, Kaye has dealt with severe trauma all by herself. She buried the incident, but the trauma cropped up in different ways in her life. She started cutting. She pulled out her hair. She started acting out with her parents. Some people resort to suicide after experiencing what Kaye did. And based on his extreme behavior, Jack has very likely hurt other children.

It's difficult to fathom everything that Kaye has been through. Her brave escape is far more than anybody should expect from most eleven-year-olds being held by twenty-six-year-olds. It is quite remarkable that she made it out alive. However, you cannot wish predators or trauma away. Trauma will continue to rear its terrible head if you do not tell someone and deal with it head-on. Thankfully, Kaye sensed that Jack could not be her boyfriend. A grown man cannot be the boyfriend of a child.

We will talk in detail about reporting, counseling, and self-care in chapter 4.

Aftermath for the Predator You can read more about predators, court proceedings, and punishments in chapter 4. There are many predator rehabilitation programs throughout the country that might be able to help someone like Jack. Many predators have been abused themselves or have psychological issues that can be treated. However, this book does not deep dive into the prison system or predator psychology. This book focuses predominantly on the victim's journey and healing.

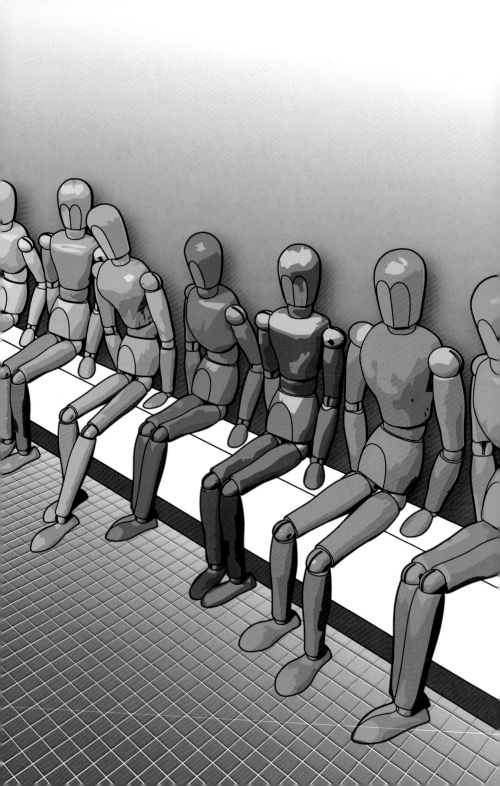

CHAPTER 3

22 MYTHS
ABOUT SEXUAL ABUSE THAT YOU SHOULD FORGET

Content warning: This chapter contains explicit sexual situations and instances of abuse and violence.

One of the best parts about #MeToo is that it's starting to shut down old myths about sexual abuse. A lot of these myths—let's call them for what they are: *lies*—are still around, and so we have a long way to go.

However, we can start by naming the myths, recognizing them, and tearing them apart one by one.

1. It's my fault if it happens to me. This is a classic myth that goes *way* back and all the way to courtrooms. When victims of sexual abuse tell their stories, they're often asked such questions as, What were you wearing at the time? Why were you at his house? You kissed boys in the past—doesn't that mean you liked it? Why didn't you fight back?

This is called **victim-blaming**, and unfortunately, many victims of all kinds of crimes blame themselves too. However, it's not their fault.

EMMA'S STORY (FICTIONAL)

One night, Emma went to the movies with her family. They came home to discover that their house had been robbed. The door was severely damaged. The family's art and jewelry were missing.

Everyone in the household was deeply traumatized. They'd lost so much, and they didn't feel safe anymore.

A few days later, their neighbor Jason came over and sat in the living room to have a chat. Emma thought Jason had come to bring snacks, to help them repair the door, and to hear their sad story. He had always been a good friend of the family.

But instead, Jason started to ask the family strange questions, such as, "Why did you go to the movies? Didn't you know that your house would be open to robbers?"

"Well, Jason," Emma's mother answered, "we thought going to the movies was okay—that our neighborhood was safe."

"You guys have this nice lawn," Jason continued. "Doesn't it attract robbers? Also, why didn't you fight back?"

"Well," Emma's dad answered, "even if we'd had the chance, they may have had guns, Jason. It could have been dangerous."

"If you ask me," Jason said, ignoring him, "you guys

asked for this."

Jason left. Emma started to wonder if he was right. Maybe it *was* the family's fault. Maybe they shouldn't feel so sorry for themselves.

Most neighbors don't react to house robberies as Jason did in this fictional story. However, they often **do** react this way when a victim says she has been assaulted, harassed, or even raped. In all of these cases, a crime has been committed. How do you think Jason **should** have reacted to the robbery? How should he react if Emma said she'd been sexually harassed at school?

2. Only strangers in alleyways do this stuff, not people I know.
In eight out of ten cases of rape, the victim knows the rapist, and 33 percent of assaults are committed by a former or current boyfriend, girlfriend, wife, or husband. The victim might trust or even love the person, which can make the abusive situation harder to leave.

3. I'm uncomfortable, but someone is telling me it's okay ... so I guess it *is* okay.
Nobody knows your body and your mind better than you do. If you're uncomfortable with a sexually charged situation or a weird relationship that's giving you the creeps, you have the right to say no and walk away, no matter what the other person says.

ROB & PRIYA'S STORY (FICTIONAL)

At school, Rob invites Priya to see a very, very scary movie in the theater. The problem is, Priya doesn't like scary movies. They make her uncomfortable and unable to sleep. She tells him that she doesn't want to go, but Rob keeps pressing: "You'll love it! You're going to be fine. I need someone to go with so I don't look lame. Seriously, you don't hate scary movies. . . . You just *think* you do."

Eventually, Priya caves. She tells herself that scary movies aren't all that bad and that she may even like it. After all, Rob is so *persistent*, and she doesn't want to upset the friendship—Rob is so cool!

So they see the movie. And guess what? Priya hates it. She's uncomfortable throughout the movie and has nightmares for months. Meanwhile, Rob goes around bragging to everyone that he saw this super-scary movie,

and, in front of everyone, he makes fun of Priya for being a scaredy-cat.

Maybe Priya will like scary movies one day, but she wasn't ready for this one. Rob wasn't committing any crime here, but he was being very selfish. He didn't listen to Priya when she said she was uncomfortable and, instead, tried to convince her that she *was* comfortable. Only Priya knows her limits, and only *you* know *your* limits, whether it's about movies, your body, or otherwise.

4. #MeToo stuff only happens to girls. Sexual abuse can happen to anyone of any gender. One in four boys will be sexually abused before they turn eighteen.

Unfortunately, a lot of boys feel so ashamed and confused by their experiences that they don't talk about them, or they blame themselves. Sexual abuse can be just as traumatic for boys, yet they are often afraid that they will appear less manly if they act like victims. They may even get erections during the abuse, which makes everything even more confusing. Regardless, they are victims too, and they are not alone.

JUSTIN'S STORY (TRUE)

When Justin Hoffmann was just seven years old, his pastor began molesting him. The abuse went on for five years. He felt ashamed and did not admit the abuse to anyone, but he suffered terrible mental health issues for decades. Thirty-eight years later, he sued the Catholic Church and told people about the abuse. He said that the #MeToo movement helped him come forward.

Justin is one of many male survivors of sexual abuse. Men and boys are not alone, even if it feels harder for them to speak up. The #MeToo movement is for everyone.

5. Attackers are never female. Anyone of any gender can also commit sexual abuse. A recent study found that 35 percent of attacks on males were committed by at least one female. Because people tend to trust women with children, it's also easier for female attackers to slip under the radar.

LAUREN'S STORY (TRUE)

Florida state senator Lauren Book wrote about her abuse at the hands of a female nanny in her memoir, *It's Ok to Tell: A Story of Hope and Recovery.*

Starting when Lauren was thirteen and until she was seventeen, her nanny Waldina raped her, beat her, threw her down a flight of stairs and, at least one time, urinated on her. All the while, Waldina had convinced Lauren that they were in love.

Because Lauren was a lonely child who was desperate for love and affection, she became dependent on her nanny and didn't want her to get in trouble. The abuse had come on slowly, but it got worse. Waldina warned Lauren not to tell anyone.

Eventually, Lauren told her parents, and Waldina fled. When authorities found her, she was volunteering for a young girls' soccer team in a different state. Finally, Waldina was arrested. Lauren has been fighting a crusade against sexual predators ever since. Still, Lauren hears this question a lot: "How does a girl get sexually abused by a woman?"

Lauren's ordeal is a case in which a woman abused a child in *exactly* the same way many predatory men do. Waldina groomed Lauren, raped her, and then escalated sexual demands, violence, and secrecy. When she was caught, she moved to a different state and put herself near young girls. This is *very* classic predatory behavior, be it a man or woman.

One thing that made Waldina even more dangerous was that she was completely undetected by other people. Nobody ever suspected a nice female nanny. So she had full private access to Lauren twenty-four hours a day.

6. Abuse doesn't even happen to LGBTQ people. Isn't it always a straight guy and a straight girl?

This might be the craziest myth of them all, because LGBTQ folks are *more* likely to be abused than any other group. Almost half (*half!*) of transgender and nonbinary people have reported sexual abuse in their lifetimes, and gay men are twice as likely to be assaulted as heterosexual men. While lesbian women are the least likely category of sexual groups to be assaulted, bisexual women are actually three times more likely to be assaulted than heterosexual women.

LGBTQ people are vulnerable to abuse (see page 29 on vulnerability) in part because they are LGBTQ. Law enforcement may not take them seriously. Some sexual attacks are also hate-based attacks.

ADELAIDE'S STORY (TRUE)

A bisexual girl named Adelaide was attacked by two straight guys in two separate incidents. In both cases, they cornered her and fondled her without her consent, completely unprompted. Both of these men knew that she was bisexual and that she preferred girls. Adelaide thinks that, in part, they attacked her because they saw her as a challenge, or perhaps they were angry because she wasn't attracted to them. Instead of dealing with their feelings, they felt the need to dominate her.

If Adelaide is correct about her attackers' motives, she has experienced two queerphobic attacks in which the attackers felt entitled to her body.

7. Gay people are definitely going to hit on me and harass me. This statement is not only untrue, it's homophobic. Gay people are *not* more inclined to abuse anyone than any other group. Unfortunately, this kind of thinking reflects what is sometimes called *gay panic*, which leads to an unfounded hatred of gay people.

8. A person will turn me gay if they abuse me. A gay abuser cannot turn a victim gay. Being gay is not something a person can pass on to someone else. The sexuality of the attacker is irrelevant to the abuse. Myths 9 and 20 touch on this further.

9. If a man abuses a boy, he must be gay. Straight men abuse boys. Straight women abuse girls. Sexual abuse isn't always about black-and-white attraction. It can be about power, control, and opportunity. (Myth 20 on this list dives into this a bit further.) The attacker's sexuality is irrelevant and should never be the main focus in an abusive situation.

10. Someone who claims to be a victim is probably lying to get attention. Yes, in rare cases, people lie about sexual abuse. Falsely accusing someone is horrible, and it's certainly not worth any attention it might afford. Not only did these false accusers ruin lives, but they made it harder for *actual* victims to be believed.

However, only 2 to 8 percent of sexual assault reports are false. That is a *very* low number. It's outrageous when people automatically assume that victims are lying.

MAXWELL'S STORY (FICTIONAL)

As soon as the school year started, a teacher emailed Maxwell, asking him how he was doing. It was kinda weird, but Maxwell didn't think much of it. After a few months, the teacher asked Maxwell to send him pictures of himself. Maxwell told his parents, who told school officials and the police. The teacher was fired and arrested.

It was a horrifying experience for Maxwell and his family, and what's worse, nobody in school believed him. Other students had loved the teacher. They gossiped, claiming that Maxwell had made it up to become popular. His sister Shana looked on with disgust. She was a few grades above Maxwell, and she wanted to protect her brother.

So Shana decided to do an experiment. She told everyone in school that she had seen Ariana Grande walking on the street the other day. Word spread. Students asked Shana about Ariana's hairdo. Her outfit. Did she sing? Who was she with? Was her voice as amazing in real life? The rumor mill got so out of control that kids started to believe Ariana had a vacation home in town.

Then Shana busted out the big guns. With Maxwell's permission, she went to Facebook and made a big announcement.

"Hey, guys. By now you've all heard the story. I mean, what are the odds that I'd meet Ariana Grande on the street?

I'll tell you. 2 percent. I did the math.

There is a 2 percent chance that Ariana Grande would be in our town, that she would take a break from her busy schedule to take a stroll on our street, and that she would bump into me. It's very, very unlikely.

So you're probably thinking that I'm super lucky. Well, I'm here to tell you that I lied. I made it up. Ariana Grande was never here.

Did you know that only about 2 percent of reported sexual abuse stories are made up? You were willing to believe the Ariana Grande story because you wanted to. Yet against reason, against all the odds, you wouldn't believe my brother."

Mic drop.

We all wish we had a sister like Shana. Why not **be** the Shana you want to see in the world? As long as the victim is okay with it, that is.

11. Boys can't help themselves, and it's up to girls to make them happy.

This is false, of course. Boys absolutely can control themselves in sexual situations, and a girl should only "make someone happy" if she wants to. No matter how much a boy may whine or persist, or even if a boy and a girl are already in a romantic relationship, a girl is under no contract to do anything she doesn't want to. This goes for all genders in all ways, gay, straight, and otherwise.

12. If someone says yes, she'll say yes every time.

This is a myth. If a girl at school hooks up with a guy, that doesn't mean she wants to hook up with *everyone*. It doesn't even mean that she'll want to hook up with the same *guy* again. Even if she says yes to a guy one minute, she can take away consent at any time.

People are complicated, and nobody should expect anything from a girl (or anyone else) just because she supposedly did something in the past.

And if she *does* want to, who cares? Don't judge people who are doing something that makes them happy. You probably don't know the full story, anyway. Not your business, move on.

13. Girls don't ever want to hook up, so they need convincing. Girls will hook up when they're ready, if they're ready. Some girls *are* into it. Maybe they're just not into it with *that* person or in *that* moment. There is nothing wrong or defective about that. "Convincing" makes it manipulative and creepy. Wouldn't it be so much more fun if *both* of you wanted to hook up with no convincing or coercion necessary? It's not a race.

PRIYA & ROB'S STORY, VERSION TWO (FICTIONAL)

Remember the story of Priya and Rob on page 74? Rob used coercion to get Priya to go to the movies. Let's consider a healthier way for that story to play out.

Rob asks Priya to see a scary movie with him. Priya says that she's uncomfortable and that scary movies give her nightmares.

"Really? Is it really that bad for you?" Rob asks.

"Yes!" she says.

"Like what? I don't get it."

"I have bad nightmares. I have them for months, and I can't fall asleep," Priya says.

"Oh, man. I guess that does sound pretty bad," Rob says. "Well, what movie do you want to see?"

"*Air Fighter 9!*" Priya yells.

"Eh, it's my second choice, but I'll go with you," he says. "I guess I can see the scary movie later."

Rob and Priya see *Air Fighter 9*, and they have a great time. After the movie, they're so excited over the special effects they can't stop talking about it. They can't wait to see another movie together. Priya thinks one day, maybe, she'll be ready for the scary movie, but there's no hurry.

In this version, Rob still wants to see the scary movie, and Priya still doesn't want to. But instead of pushing her to do something she doesn't want to do, he asks her questions about her feelings, and he listens to her. He is able to work within her limits, even though they are very different from his. They both have a better time and a better connection. This is an example of good communication.

14. If people just learned self-defense moves, this wouldn't happen. Apologies if you're a superhero movie fan, but this book isn't going to get into self-defense moves or fighting. Plenty of other books, resources, and classes are

about physical self-defense. They are very useful and empowering, and I encourage every reader to look into them. Fitness is great. Knowing some moves could come in handy one day.

However, learning self-defense is *not enough* to stop sexual abuse, and stopping abuse should not be the responsibility of victims and their allies. The abuser should not abuse at all.

This myth has led to some very bad decisions and serious victim-blaming. In one famous 2014 case, a Canadian judge asked a teenage rape victim, "Why couldn't you just keep your knees together?" He then ruled in favor of the alleged rapist.

This judge didn't only seem to have a weird idea of how the human body is shaped, but he basically blamed the girl for being raped because she did not practice self-defense. If she had known a jujitsu move to pin the guy down, that might have been handy, but it's not her legal responsibility to know and use jujitsu. Also, it doesn't mean that the jujitsu would have worked. What if the attacker had had a gun? What if he was much, much stronger than her?

It also doesn't mean the attack didn't happen. It still happened. It should not have happened. It is the responsibility of the rapist *not to rape*, and it is the authorities' responsibility to *protect victims*. It is not the responsibility of victims to learn self-defense, even if it's handy.

15. I can't relax, because I'll be accused of harassment.
As more and more men were accused of sexual abuse during the height of #MeToo, some boys and their parents became afraid. They believed that they couldn't relax or be themselves because any minute, they'd be accused of sexual abuse. If they talked to a girl, they'd be accused of harassment. If they accidentally looked at one, they'd be accused of rape.

As you learned from myth 10, only 2 to 8 percent of rape or harassment accusations are false. That's a *very low* percentage. If you don't rape, harass, abuse, stalk, or coerce, you'll be just fine.

Refer to chapter 2 for definitions of sexually abusive behaviors.

16. The victim didn't say anything to teachers or police right away, so it probably didn't happen.
Three out of four sexual assaults go unreported and, unfortunately, for good reason. Reporting harassment, assault, or abuse of any kind can be very scary. Sometimes the victims believe the act is their fault (see myth 1). Sometimes they don't want to get the abuser in trouble or they don't trust their teachers or police or they don't think anyone will believe them.

They may fear **retaliation**—when an abuser seeks revenge on an accuser, perhaps by spreading lies about the accuser. Sometimes, reporting can make things even harder on the victim than the abuser.

AMBER'S STORY (TRUE)

In 2007 two male classmates raped Amber Wyatt, a high school student, in a shed. She reported the incident to police. A ton of physical evidence confirmed that she had been raped.

However, when police questioned everyone involved, including thirty-five classmates and adults, nobody backed her up. Almost all of them defended the boys' side of the story. After all, these boys were well-liked soccer players. They painted Amber as a "whore" and a drug addict, even graffitiing horrible words about her on walls and cars. Everyone in town found out about her private life and openly made fun of her. The case never went to trial, and nobody was prosecuted for the rape. Amber switched schools, but the events still haunt her.

Amber Wyatt's case is extreme, and sympathy toward victims has improved somewhat since #MeToo, but it's no wonder that so many assaults go unreported. If a victim refuses to report it, that does *not* mean the account is untrue. A victim may just be fearful of the consequences, and rightfully so.

17. It's only real if it's outright molestation or rape.

Most of the abuse cases we hear about are very violent or creepy stories about rape and molestation. These kinds of stories get the top headlines because they're very clear-cut: there's a hero and a villain, and the salacious details are straight out of a movie.

However, if this is the only type of abuse that we talk about, then #MeToo hasn't done its job. It means that other forms of abuse don't feel "legitimate."

Most sexual abuse *isn't* as clear-cut or wild as those headlines. It can come as texts. It can be a hidden dynamic between a boyfriend and a girlfriend or two boyfriends. It can come on very slowly and gradually. It can take on many forms, and sometimes the details can feel murky. That doesn't make the abuse any less real.

18. Abuse is only between an adult and a kid.

Nope. Peer abuse is very real and scary. And 40 percent of victims have been abused by an older or more powerful child. Often it's harder for adults to respond or recognize peer abuse, because they can't tell the difference between abuse and adolescent curiosity. Turn to page 48 for a more detailed definition of peer abuse.

19. I can easily spot an abuser.

It's not always obvious that someone is an abuser. Very few abusers wear scary masks or skulk around in the dark. Many of them seem super nice at first.

Often abusers have personal issues. Abusers are often victims or survivors themselves. They might be getting abused at home. They might be acting out. They may have mental illnesses that make it difficult for them to respect boundaries. (Borderline personality disorder, or BPD, is a potential example, but not all people with BPD abuse others.) You *can* spot an abuser, but not by their looks, position, clothes, race, class, sexuality, disposition, or personality disorder. Unfortunately, you have to get to know them a bit.

Here are some signs, or red flags, that you're dealing with an older abuser:

He does not respect boundaries or listen when someone tells him no.

She engages in touching even though a kid has said no.

He tries to be a kid's friend rather than filling an adult role. (This might feel cool, but it can be a sign of predatory behavior.)

She offers a kid drugs, alcohol, pornography, or other inappropriate things.

They do not seem to have healthy relationships with people their own age.

He insists on keeping secrets with kids.

They talk with kids about their personal problems or relationships.

She spends time alone with children outside of her role in a kid's life or makes up excuses to be alone with a child.

He expresses unusual interest in a kid's sexual development, such as commenting on sexual characteristics or sexualizing normal behaviors.

She gives a child gifts without occasion or good reason. (Most adults outside of families shouldn't be giving individual children gifts.)

Other signs of an abuser—an older one or a peer—include the following:

She targets a vulnerable victim who has low self-esteem.

People really like him, because he is outgoing and funny.

She's a narcissist, or she has an exaggerated opinion of herself and consistently puts herself above everyone else.

He acts as though he really likes someone one minute and then mistreats them the next.

They engage in risky behavior, such as driving really fast to scare a victim, cutting class, or doing drugs or alcohol.

She tends to be extremely oversensitive, seeing every interaction or event as a personal attack.

He consistently pushes sexual boundaries and asks for things over and over, even if another person has said no.

She blames others for her problems.

He puts the responsibility for his feelings and needs on other people instead of on himself, which leads to unreasonable expectations. For example, he might say, "You gave me a hard-on, so you have to finish or you'll make me really upset."

She displays cruelty toward animals or younger children.

In a close relationship, an abuser might use some of the following techniques:

He starts a relationship with intense flattery and then insists that things get very serious very quickly.

She isolates a victim from friends or family.

He doesn't seem to care much about a victim's feelings unless he absolutely has to.

She acts jealous or controlling, which can seem like love and care at the beginning of a relationship. But it's not.

He expects a victim to make him feel better and tend to all his needs.

She pushes sexual boundaries . . . and then pushes them more and more.

He uses sexual activity such as spanking or hurting to demean a victim.

He uses verbal abuse, such as insulting a victim's looks.

She goes back and forth between being nice and being abusive.

If a victim tries to leave, he begs, pleads, and gets extremely emotional.

She makes violent threats or uses violence and then attempts to justify doing so.

He causes worry in a victim's family and friends, but then he tries to push these people out of the victim's life.

20. A person in my life is abusive according to some stuff in this book, but they need me. I can help them. It's true that abusers are often victims themselves. However, even if an abuser is a victim, that does not make abuse okay, and it does not mean that a victim is obligated to obey, pity, or fix an abuser. Therapy should be left to professionals, and victims should protect themselves first and foremost. No matter what an abuser says, a nonprofessional cannot help or fix someone, and victims will suffer if they try.

21. Abusers are so sexually attracted to victims that they just can't help themselves. Sure, an abuser might be sexually attracted to a victim. However, this myth has a very negative effect. It might, for example, encourage people to blame a victim for being *so attractive* or for wearing an outfit that's *so sexy* that an abuser just had to engage in abuse. This does not happen, and the abuser is responsible for their behavior, not the other way around.

You can be *very* sexually attracted to someone and *not* abuse them, so sexual attraction is not the only thing happening in an abusive situation. An abuser is acting on other impulses.

Other factors at play might be a need for power and control, a lack of empathy, or an opportunity.

Over the past few years, many accusers have come out against the Catholic Church. Many men say that as young boys, they were groomed and abused by priests. These crimes do not imply that *all* the abusing priests were gay or intensely attracted to boys in general.

According to records, some Catholic priests used their authority and knowledge of biblical scripture to bully, threaten, and coerce children into doing what they wanted. This demonstrates a need for power and control.

The priests did not recognize or care that their actions would traumatize the boys. This shows a lack of empathy, or ability to care about someone else's feelings.

These priests had constant access to young, vulnerable boys whom they could exploit in secret. This was opportunity.

Sexual attraction is quite separate from these things.

22. I've been sexually abused, or I know someone who has. There's nothing I can do. You can fight back. Whether the abuser is a family member, a pastor, a friend, or anyone in your life, you have power, and you don't deserve to suffer. Chapter 4 goes into detail about where to turn.

If you know someone who's been hurt, you can be an **ally**, or a person who supports sexual abuse victims. Chapter 5 discusses how to be an ally.

Even if you've never encountered abuse, you can help spread awareness and the #MeToo message. Turn to chapter 6 to learn more.

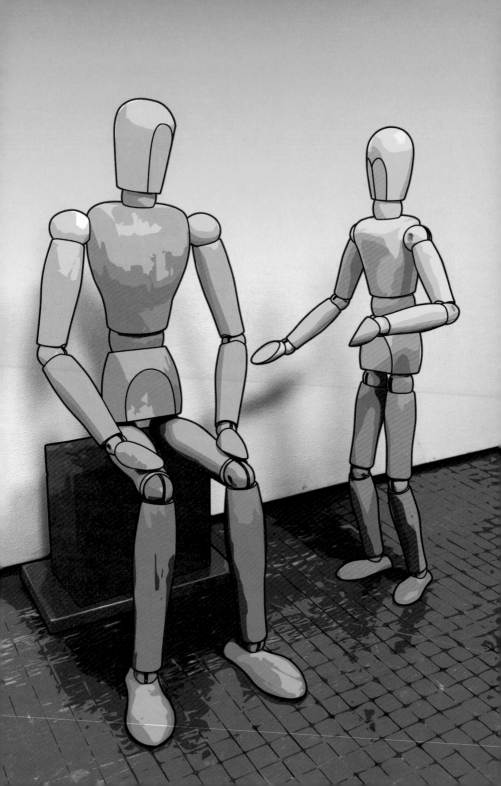

CHAPTER 4

ASKING FOR HELP

Content warning: This chapter contains sexually explicit content and potentially triggering content.

Asking for help can be very difficult. Here are some reasons why many victims don't pursue outside support:

Victims fear retaliation from their abusers.

They don't trust authorities to fix the problem or to keep them safe.

They feel as if the incident wasn't "bad" enough to report.

They don't think anyone will believe them.

They don't understand that it's abuse because the abusers have influenced their thinking.

They feel as if it's all their fault.

It feels as if it's just not worth the trouble.

Because of these reasons and more, only 38 percent of child abuse victims say *anything*, and about 40 percent of *those* kids only tell their friends, not grown-ups. This means a majority of child sex abuse cases go unreported and unaddressed, and a huge number of predators are still free.

Abuse is never a victim's fault, and many levels of abuse deserve attention, no matter how bad—or not bad—they seem.

However, other notes on the list above are very valid. Sometimes abusers really *do* retaliate against a victim. Worse, sometimes authorities fail.

I wish that I could tell you that reporting abuse is always a perfectly gratifying experience and that everything will work out exactly the way you want—the villains will get punished accordingly, justice will be served, and the victim will feel fantastic and move on. Unfortunately, that doesn't always happen. Justice is not always served. Perpetrators do not always get what's coming to them. The system is flawed in handling these things, and sometimes, the victim suffers.

It takes a *lot* of bravery to ask for help. When you're an adult, you usually get to decide whether to press charges against an abuser. However, if you're a kid and you tell an authority about an abuse you suffered, the information will probably automatically get reported to others. Your school, law enforcement, and possibly other child protective agencies might get involved. This commitment is often filled with pressure and doubt.

But not always. Most adults want to protect children. Most people want to help and see bad situations dealt with properly. Many resources are available to child victims and their families.

If most adults had their way, there would be no more sex abuse anywhere. Even if reporting can be flawed some-times, a ton of support is out there. Open arms are waiting to extract victims from their situations and get them the help and counseling they need. Abuse should never, ever fall on the shoulders of a victim alone.

If a victim is armed with information, he or she can enter the reporting situation prepared. If victims are prepared and have folks in their corner, then weighing their options and telling people they trust *can* be a gratifying experience, and the victim can heal.

The victim might also save others from the same suffering.

This chapter will not sugarcoat the difficulties in report-ing, but it will discuss how to seek help in a way that can benefit a victim. It will show you what to expect when you tell a teacher, a parent, or a friend. We'll explain what hap-pens when you take abuse to court and when an abuser gets convicted. You'll learn some legal stuff that you don't have to memorize, but it's very handy to have it somewhere in the back of your mind.

For the sake of making this easy to read and understand, I'll sometimes refer to a victim as "you" throughout this chapter. This does *not* mean that you, the reader, are a victim of abuse. The "you" might refer to somebody you know or even someone you *don't* know.

THE DANGERS OF NOT ASKING FOR HELP

If asking for help can cause problems, the dangers of not asking for help are far worse. Those possible dangers include the following:

The abuse will continue, escalate, or both.

You will live with unexamined trauma, which can affect you psychologically for the rest of your life.

Trauma, when untreated, can cause severe issues, including depression, anxiety, relationship trouble, drug and alcohol problems, and suicidal tendencies.

The abuser may harm other victims.

Reporting is hard, but you don't need to endure all of this alone.

HOW TO SEEK HELP

Step 1. Admit you need help. This can be one of the toughest steps. It's easier to tell yourself that a situation is not that bad, that you can handle it alone, and that admitting it's a problem will only make things worse. Admitting you need help is especially difficult if the abuser is consistently in your life and telling you lies.

Remember that things will only get worse for you if you don't get help. Possibly, the abuse will end on its own, but you will be left carrying the trauma (see page 64). Even the toughest people in the world can't do that by themselves.

Step 2. Know the lowdown on physical evidence.

Most child sexual abuse cases carry little to no physical evidence. However, if there *is* physical evidence, victims may help their cases later on by keeping it around.

Physical evidence can include notes, emails, photos, or texts between the abuser and the victim. Knowing if there were any witnesses may help.

If the abuse is violent, physical evidence can include bruises or cuts. Take clear photos of this evidence along with distinct markings (such as your face or a birthmark) to prove the lacerations are yours.

If you have been sexually assaulted, a doctor can administer a rape kit exam, which is an invasive physical exam of the entire body. Collecting this evidence may help identify the abuser and prove that an assault has occurred. A rape kit examination can only be administered within seventy-two hours after the assault. The victim cannot shower before the test and is encouraged to wear the same clothes worn during the assault. The victim should wait to wash anything that may be used as evidence, including clothes or bedsheets.

It's easy to see why very little physical evidence is associated with child abuse cases. Victims can feel embarrassed by texts, emails, or pictures, so they delete them instead of saving them. If they have been hurt by somebody they know, they often don't want to go to the hospital to get a rape kit exam or to have bruises examined. Also, an abuser does not always leave marks.

Step 3. After a crisis, remember these things.

Abuse will throw your life for a loop.

The abuse does not define you. You are still yourself.

Abuse does not mean that you're abnormal all of a sudden. You are overcoming a terrible challenge, but you are not weird.

Nobody knows about the abuse unless someone witnessed it or unless you tell someone. You are not wearing it on your shirt.

Resuming a normal life is your ultimate goal, when you are ready.

Step 4. Remember the facts with care. If you report
the abuse to the authorities, they will ask for details of what happened, probably more than once. If you wind up taking the abuse to court, you'll be asked for the facts many, many times. While professionals usually guide kids through this process, it

can still be very difficult. Trauma can cause lapses in memory, which means you may forget pieces of the events. It can feel very painful and difficult to recall these things to strangers. When you are ready and have adequate support, these are the questions that authorities may ask:

Who committed the abuse?

What date or dates did the abuse happen?

If it happened many times, can you remember when it started? Maybe the year? Is there an event, such as a holiday, close to that time that you can remember?

Where did the abuse happen?

Has there been physical contact? If so, where did the person touch you?

How did they touch you (penetration, stroking, or hitting)?

Is there physical evidence, such as bruising?

Are there witnesses?

Have you told anyone?

Was there sexual, verbal, or digital contact? What did the person say, text, or email?

Do you have any records of your conversations— emails, calls, or texts—and if so, can you put them in a single place?

Remember, there are no wrong or right answers to these questions—you just need the truth.

Step 5. Tell someone, even if you're unsure about proof. I've talked a little about physical evidence and witnesses in this chapter, and if these things are available to you, they could be very helpful later. However, it is way more important that you tell an adult that you are being abused so that you can be safe and get the help you need. Do not let a lack of proof stop you. It is not your responsibility to prove things. You are not a lawyer, a detective, or a prosecutor. By listing steps 2 and 3 above, I am hoping to prepare victims for what might come when they tell an adult, but do not stress too much about proof, especially in a crisis.

Step 6. Know the definitions. Very few people falsely report abuse, but some children report incorrect facts because of their lack of knowledge, according to Cheryl Graf, a doctor who works for Stop Sexual Assault in Schools.

Before you use words like *rape* and *molestation*, for example, be sure you know what those words mean. It might be more accurate if you describe the activity, by saying something like: "He texted me sexual words" or "She grabbed my breasts with her hands."

You can refer back to chapter 2 for definitions.

Step 7. Tell a trusted adult. Your peers don't have the power or knowledge to help you. Your siblings and same-age cousins don't either. The best a kid can do is tell an adult.

So choose a trusted adult. This must be someone who is protective of you, who cares about you, and who can take action so that you don't have to carry this burden by yourself. You should know this person very well. A lot of kids choose to tell their parents. Others may tell teachers, coaches, or doctors.

Can you think of any adults in your life who fit this description?

Step 8. If you don't have an adult you trust, tell someone else. If you don't feel comfortable telling any adults in your life, there are organizations that can help you.

You can call national hotlines, including the following:

National Sexual Assault Hotline (coordinated by the Rape, Abuse & Incest National Network, or RAINN), (800) 656-HOPE

Darkness to Light, (866) FOR-LIGHT or text LIGHT to 741741

There is also 911.

All of these numbers have trained professionals ready to help. They will be able to support you emotionally and connect you with the proper resources in your area. Bear in mind that these professionals are usually bound by mandatory reporting (see step 9) when a child is involved. If you are in immediate danger in your home, for example, they might alert your local child services to investigate your home situation.

More hotlines and resources are listed in the Additional Resources section.

Step 9. Learn about mandatory reporting. Some adults in your life are bound by mandatory reporting—if you tell them you've been abused, they *have* to tell the authorities. It's the law. So, if you report abuse to someone, the report will probably reach the next rung in the ladder. If you tell a teacher, for example, the teacher may have to tell law enforcement and the school principal.

If the act is criminal, law enforcement will get involved. Peer abuse often remains a school issue. (See page 122.)

A doctor might be obligated to tell Child Protective Services (a government organization), depending on state laws. If you tell a person on a hotline (see step 8), they are obligated to tell authorities as well. To find out who in your state is bound by mandatory reporting, visit the Child Welfare Information Gateway at https://www.childwelfare.gov /topics/systemwide/laws-policies/statutes/manda/.

The first person you contact is not necessarily responsible for investigating the incident and seeking justice, but they must report it.

Your parents and relatives are not bound by mandatory reporting. It is unlikely that your parents and relatives will know exactly what to do when you tell them you were abused. Sadly, adults are typically not educated about this stuff until it happens to their kids. However, it is their responsibility to become educated and to protect you. The adults in your life can learn more about mandatory reporting at https://www.childwelfare.gov/.

Step 10. Know that adults have emotional reactions too.
When a child reports abuse to an adult, the adult is encouraged to do three things:

Listen to the victim and find out the facts.

Say, "I believe you."

Stay calm and be supportive. Do *not* freak out, go ballistic, or start threatening violence against the abuser, especially not around the victim.

These are the guidelines that adults *should* follow. Unfortunately, not all adults know these guidelines, and this book isn't written for them. (Feel free to show this section to the trusted adults in your life, though!)

If an adult freaks out, remember that you did not do *anything* wrong by speaking up. This person is probably having a very emotional reaction because they care so much about you. It may feel as though you are responsible for setting something negative in motion. However, the abuser did that, *not you*. You are also not responsible for the trusted adult's reaction. That person is a grown-up, responsible for handling their own emotions and doing the right thing.

(To be honest, I would have a hard time holding in my anger if my daughter told me she had been abused. However, even if I didn't react perfectly right away, that wouldn't stop me from taking the action necessary to protect her.)

If an adult does not believe you or if he or she dismisses you, that will be very discouraging. If you're in the unfortunate position of being in a family that doesn't have your well-being in mind, don't give up. Choose a different adult.

Step 11. Seek counseling and self-care. Sex abuse victims must go to counseling immediately after a crisis.

It is very important for victims to take care of themselves. Victims endure so much stress that without counseling, terrible consequences may occur. Stress sometimes escalates during the reporting process, so it's even more important then.

Stress and abuse trauma take a major toll on the body and mind. They can lead to poor sleep, bad eating habits, skin problems, poor school performance, depression, anxiety, and more. In acute cases, stress can lead to self-harm, relationship trouble, drug and alcohol abuse, and more.

Counseling is a must, and the adults in your life should confer to get you the best care possible immediately after a crisis.

You can also talk to your school guidance counselor about options.

With the right help, you can heal. It will take time, but you can also get lifelong benefits from counseling. It leads to better mental health and important tools for your whole life, not just after a crisis.

Finally, you *must* seek and accept love and support. Gather your loved ones. Talk about your feelings with them. Let them take care of you. Cry on them. Tell them what you need. Or tell them that you don't know *what* you need but that you just want them around, or you need them on the phone, even if they're not saying anything. If they love you, they will oblige. Withdrawing will only deepen terrible feelings and stress. Being open will allow you to heal.

To optimize healing, you will need to exercise. Being sedentary will increase feelings of depression and anxiety. Exercise will help boost your confidence, improve your mood, decrease your stress, help you eat better, and regain your relationship with your body. The benefits are endless. You don't have to be a powerlifter or a marathon runner. Just thirty minutes of exercise, even just brisk walking, each day will make a huge difference.

If possible, take some breaks from the proceedings when you need to. Tell your caregivers that you don't want to talk about the abuse incident today or that you don't want to talk to social workers—that you just want it to be a normal day. Maybe suggest a nice dinner out with the family or a trip somewhere. The abuse happened, but it isn't your whole life. You are allowed to take breaks, as long as you don't bury it deep and forget it happened.

Healing is ongoing, but you *will* break out of crisis mode with the right support. These self-care tips will serve you throughout your life.

Step 12. Stay safe and report retaliation.

If you've reported abuse, nobody is allowed to retaliate against you. Read more about retaliation on page 63.

If anyone is retaliating or making you feel uncomfortable for reporting the incident or incidents, tell your trusted adult. If your abuser is not supposed to contact you and does anyway, try to document the incident and tell your adult right away. As long as you can ignore the abuser safely, do so. Do not engage with the abuser.

Step 13. Remember, your anonymity is legally protected.

Your name should never be publicly revealed—not in court documents, not in reports, and certainly not in newspapers. The federal rape shield law protects your anonymity.

Heads up: Steps 14 through 19 involve the law. Remember, it's not your burden to memorize all of this stuff, but it is useful information for anyone seeking justice for sexual abuse. Most grown-ups aren't aware of these options, either, so this is a great starting point for all of you.

Step 14. Get your school's Title IX policy, and track down the Title IX officer.

If the abuse occurred at school, or at the hands of a school official . . .
If your school abides by Title IX, it has a policy against sexual harassment in its Title IX documents. You should be able

to get a copy of the Title IX policy to review your rights. Your school also has a Title IX officer or coordinator, who could be anyone from a guidance counselor to a vice principal. Track down the representative, and ask questions about investigative policies, filing complaints, and anything else you might be worried about. Bring your trusted adult if you'd like. A Title IX officer often has the authority to issue a "no contact" rule between you and your abuser.

Step 15. Take precautions with online research.

You may choose to search online for answers or support. The internet can be an incredible resource, but when looking up answers about legal issues, counseling, mental health, abuse, and highly sensitive topics, take some precautions.

Never give out your information online. If you wish to speak with someone about your situation, call one of the confidential hotlines listed in step 8 or in the Additional Resources section at the end of this book. Don't just call any number you find, and don't input your information anywhere.

Websites that end in .gov or .edu are by far the most reliable. However, many great organizations use .org as well. Please refer to the Additional Resources section for a list of useful websites. Don't stray too far from that list.

Don't ask for any information on social media, and if you have a legal case pending, don't talk about it at all online. Your friends don't have the expertise to help you, and public posts may affect your case.

If you're looking for real information, stay away from discussion boards where anyone can sound off. Reddit discussions, Quora, and 4Chan are not helpful.

If you are reading news articles, listicles, first-person stories, or advice, make sure they are published in real, credible publications. Credible articles cite real studies and research, or they use real quotes from experts, such as doctors or lawyers. Still, in today's landscape it can be hard to discern real information from fake. Be cautious when researching articles.

A *lot* of negativity is on the internet, and it can be particularly hard to ignore this negativity if you're in an emotional place and searching for answers. You may see anonymous trolls saying that victims deserve abuse, websites dedicated to demeaning women, or just off-color comments that trigger you. It's impossible to filter the flow of information and negativity online, so be cautious, and try to remember that internet negativity is *not* reality.

If you find information online that might be relevant to your situation, tell your trusted adult. Researching on the internet might be a comfort to you, but it should not be your number one source of information or aid.

Step 16. File a complaint with a government agency.

If nothing happens after complaining to school officials . . .

You or your parents can file a complaint against the school with the US Department of Education's Office for Civil Rights (OCR). Generally, you must file a complaint with the OCR within 180 days of an act of discrimination or harassment. To find the contact information for your local OCR office, visit the agency's website at http://wdcrobcolp01.ed.gov/CFAPPS /OCR/contactus.cfm.

Step 17. Talk to a lawyer.

If things have escalated beyond filing a complaint . . .

Parents or caregivers usually hire lawyers on behalf of a child abuse victim. A good lawyer will help you navigate your issue and figure out if you have a case. Talking to a lawyer doesn't mean that you're automatically going to court. It might just mean you're getting information.

Your parents or caregivers should look for a lawyer who specializes in working with abuse trauma victims. A lawyer with this particular set of skills will know the law, know how to talk to a victim of trauma, and know about all the trauma resources in your area.

If a parent or caregiver is the abuser, a child can get help from social workers, child advocates, and if necessary, a guardian ad litem, or an attorney appointed by the court to protect a child.

Step 18. Learn what to expect in court proceedings.

Sexual abuse court proceedings are nothing like what you see in the movies. In court you can file a civil suit, which might get the victim monetary damages (a.k.a. money). Another option is to pursue criminal charges, which might sentence the abuser to fines, prison time, or juvenile detention time if the abuser is a minor.

If you are a victim, I do not want to dissuade you from going to court and seeking justice to the fullest extent. But for the sake of being realistic, it's important to understand a few things about pressing charges in our court system.

Court proceedings can take a lot of time. It could be years before you get any results.

Court proceedings don't necessarily help you move on. They may drag, frustrate you, and stress you out.

This is a sad truth, but in our court system, it often takes money, connections, and many loud, consistent adult advocates to get things moving and to get people interested.

It is very common for cases never to reach court for many reasons. A case might be settled out of court. Then the victim gets a money settlement from the school or abuser. Or county prosecutors can decide not to take a case for any reason.

Abusers often don't pay settlements they owe because they often don't have enough money.

Peer-to-peer sexual violence is criminally prosecuted very infrequently. Most often a victim will sue the school system responsible. See Carrie Goldberg's story below, and turn to page 122 for more information on peer abuse.

Some crimes have a statute of limitations—if you wait for a certain amount of time, the abuser can't be punished. The statute of limitations is different in each state and for each crime. Texas has no statute of limitations for "indecent acts on children." In Idaho, however, "sexual exploitation of a child" has a five-year statute of limitations. That means that if you're from Idaho, you have five years after a crime to report it or else it can't go to court. To find out your state's statute of limitations laws, visit RAINN's interactive tool at https://www.rainn.org/statutes-limitations.

CARRIE GOLDBERG'S STORY (TRUE)

Here are two real-life court cases involving peer-to-peer sex abuse.

A group of boys forced a mentally impaired girl into a stairwell at their school in New York and forced her to perform oral sex on them. She told the school administrators, who allegedly framed the act as consensual, and they suspended *her* for committing sex acts in school. The girl hired a lawyer and sued the school for discrimination and Title IX violation. The case did not go to trial, but the girl was awarded $950,000 from the school district. One of the boys was charged with sexual assault and misconduct.

The victim's lawyer for that case, Carrie Goldberg, is still fighting another case, in which a classmate raped a thirteen-year-old girl in an alleyway and then distributed a video of the attack around school, where the victim was bullied and taunted. A school counselor told the girl to move on with her life. School officials told her to leave school for a while, because her presence was making everything worse. She missed four months of school. When the girl attempted to return to school, she was told that the video "looked consensual." The attacker complained to police that his reputation was being ruined. For this horrific treatment, she is suing the school district.

Goldberg said that it's very hard to get peer-to-peer abusers prosecuted.

In the second case, schools might suspend or expel the

offenders, but as minors, the offenders are protected by privacy laws, and so Goldberg has no idea what happened to any of the rapists. Neither does the victim.

In the first case, you can argue that the victim got something close to justice. She got a lot of money, and one of the boys was charged criminally. It's likely that the other boys were expelled or suspended, but we'll never know.

It's yet to be seen if the victim in the second case will get any justice.

That said, no court battle can erase the damage that has been done or the years that have been taken from victims' lives. During the time they should have been learning and being normal kids, they were suffering from PTSD (post-traumatic stress disorder) and talking to lawyers. They hadn't done a thing to bring this on themselves, and most of the rapists were not criminally prosecuted. The girls in these cases deserve every ounce of justice they can get. However, I don't want to give the impression that these proceedings can eliminate the pain or get a victim everything he or she wants.

Step 19. File a lawsuit against the school. Let's say you want to go the civil suit route (step 17). You can file a lawsuit against a school if officials have been negligent in defending your Title IX rights. But you must do it quickly, because there are time limits for filing a lawsuit. States' time limits vary from one to six years. Your parents or guardians can consult an attorney for more information.

Step 20. File an order of protection, a.k.a. a restraining order. You can file a restraining order—also called an order of protection—against an abuser if they've been charged with a crime. Compared to court proceedings, which take a long time, this can be done relatively quickly through the police. The restraining order might instruct the abuser not to come near you, your family, or your school, depending on the situation. If the abuser violates a restraining order, he or she is committing a crime and could be arrested.

Step 21. Let the adults handle it, and try to resume your life. Once you've spoken up and given the facts, your responsibility is basically over. You may be asked for the facts a few more times, and you also need to stay vigilant when it comes to retaliation, but you do not have to do anything beyond this. The case is handed over to professionals.

This may be a relief on some level, but it can also be frustrating and scary for a victim. Things move slowly. You might not get justice quickly. Everything is moving out of your control. What started as an interaction between you and one other person (the abuser) has become a firestorm of activity involving school officials, lawyers, doctors, social workers, and more. You might sit in a courtroom right away or never see a courtroom at all. Many more rules and officials are involved than you ever thought possible.

Frustrating as it is, it is up to your adult advocates to fight for you. Do not take the law into your hands by, say, contacting the abuser. It will not help, and it may wind up hurting you.

Following protocol is very important. It is the only chance of getting justice, protection, and care.

This may require a lot of self-restraint. You will probably be advised not to discuss the situation much with friends, and not at all on social media. You may not be allowed to contact the abuser and vice versa. All of this may feel terrible and difficult, but it's in the interest of keeping you and your case safe, if you decide to move forward with a case.

The adults will handle it. All they want is for you to try to resume a normal life.

GIANNA & MR. DENSCH'S STORY, PART TWO (TRUE)

You read about Gianna and her teacher Mr. Densch on page 42.
Here's what happened next.

Gianna and her friends marched straight into the principal's office to tell him about Mr. Densch's behavior. They liked and trusted their principal, Mr. Fleiss.

The five girls sat across from Mr. Fleiss and proceeded to unload everything. The period bathroom thing, the standing-too-close thing, his strictness lately, the arm-grabbing thing, and some more stuff they hadn't discussed before. For example, one of Gianna's friends mentioned that Mr. Densch's shirts were always dirty and that he smelled.

This was a lot for Mr. Fleiss to take in. The girls were understandably agitated. He said to them, "Let's talk about which things are actually actionable and which things are just venting."

Mr. Fleiss and the girls broke down each of the accusations. The dirty shirt thing, for example, would not be part of a report. But the period thing was not okay.

Gianna asked if they could all just sit down with Mr. Densch with Mr. Fleiss present and talk things over. Mr. Fleiss said he would love to, but it was against the rules. He would have to report the actionable behavior to the Department of Education. He said that he wasn't sure how to categorize it since it didn't exactly fall under harassment but that he would make a report.

Gianna groaned. She didn't want Mr. Densch to get in trouble. It felt way overblown. She started to have regrets. She and her friends had come in half-cocked and emotional, and now the Department of Education was involved? It was so awkward. Couldn't Mr. Fleiss just make it stop and everyone could move on?

But that's not how it works.

Mr. Fleiss talked to every girl's parents separately to discuss the issue. The girls were told not to talk about it in school, but everybody found out anyway. Gianna was still in Mr. Densch's class for a few more months, which was so awkward. But she did notice that his behavior started to get better. He stopped being so strict. He stopped trying to be chummy with the kids.

Mr. Fleiss told the parents that the Department of Education had launched an investigation. Months later, they called Gianna to quiz her on the details of Mr. Densch's behavior. By then all of the girls had moved on. Gianna was annoyed that she still had to talk about it.

A year later, Gianna still hadn't found out exactly what happened. Mr. Densch still worked at the school, but Gianna no longer took his class. She waved hello to him in the hallway, and he waved back.

So, was it worth it? Yes and no. Mr. Densch had been acting really weird, and Gianna was no longer comfortable in his class. Something had to be done. If not for her, then for future students. She still wished that she and her friends hadn't been so emotional when they had gone in to talk to Mr. Fleiss and that they'd gone in with a more coherent plan. She was unhappy with how she had presented herself. She still wished that she could have just sat down with Mr. Densch and Mr. Fleiss instead of letting the problem get so big.

Yes, this is an unsatisfying story. We want closure. However, this is a great, true example of how sometimes, you **don't** get closure. We do know that a report was made, that an investigation was launched, and that Mr. Fleiss followed protocol. We also know that Mr. Densch's behavior wasn't easily definable by the school system. It's not criminal activity either.

Sitting down with Mr. Densch and discussing the problem may feel like a good idea to Gianna, but it's against the rules for a reason. When inappropriate behavior between a teacher and a student is reported, it is considered very serious. Schools get sued over this stuff. Teachers get fired. Students get traumatized. An unmonitored, informal chat between the students and

Mr. Densch could have major consequences. As frustrating as it is, there is a reason why a strict, boring, bureaucratic system of accountability and reports exists.

If Mr. Densch's behavior had been more severe (like an assault or harassment), Gianna **might** have seen faster and more transparent results. It's also possible that if the girls had continued to push the issue instead of dropping it, Gianna would have gotten more information. But this is all just speculation.

The main problem **did** seem to go away. The adults handled it, in the sense that Gianna and her friends weren't really burdened or involved beyond stating the facts. It was awkward for a while, but Gianna is now in a safe and happy school environment. That's all Mr. Fleiss ever wanted for her.

22. Tell your friends (maybe). Your friends won't know about the abuse unless they are witnesses. The abuse is not written on your forehead. If you want them to know, you can tell them, but you don't have to.

If you tell a friend, make sure that you're very explicit about secrecy. Be very clear about who you want your friend to tell or not tell. Unfortunately, even the most trustworthy friends might crack. It's very hard for kids in middle school to keep secrets. So tell friends at your own risk. Also, don't expect them to say all the right things. They're young and probably inexperienced with being allies.

Everything here applies to every gender identity.

All of the above applies to male-identifying and nonbinary

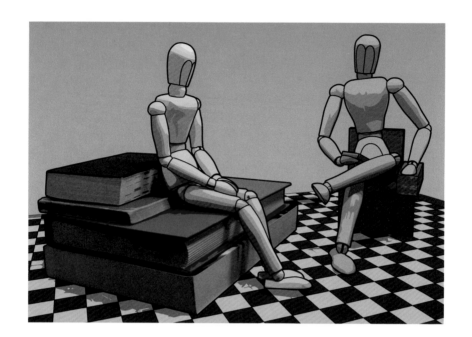

kids as well as girls, including trans students. Boys may feel as if they can't be open about their emotions or report abuse because it's not considered manly. However, boys are prone to the same consequences if they don't seek help and express themselves.

THE AFTERMATH

What are the consequences for the perpetrator?

There is a *very* wide range of consequences for convicted abusers, so it's important not to get hung up on one consequence or one track. Not everyone goes to jail, for example. The following is a *very* general overview:

If the perpetrator is an adult . . .

The consequences depend on the nature of the abuse, who

committed it, and where they committed it.

In some cases, such as Gianna's story on page 116, the issue is handled by the school with no law enforcement involved. The perpetrator may be ordered to take special classes or to undergo treatment. If the perpetrator is a known problem, that person might lose a job or a teaching license.

If the law is involved and the abuser is *convicted*, or found guilty, of sexual abuse against a child, he or she may face fines and imprisonment, according to US law. The penalties will be harsher if the crime was *aggravated*, meaning that the perpetrator used force or threats, inflicted serious bodily injury or death, or kidnapped a child to commit the abuse.

The national sex offender registry lists convicted abusers and information about them. The registry is meant to be a safety measure for the public, but it's also considered a punishment for the people on the list, since they are publicly marked and will have difficulty finding a job or resuming a normal life. The offenses on this list have ranged widely, from human trafficking to a seventeen-year-old boy who had consensual sex with his fifteen-year-old girlfriend. The national sex offender registry is at https://www.nsopw.gov/.

If an abuser commits acts against his or her own children or wards, social services might take away those kids and hold them in a safe place, such as a relative's house or in a group home for children.

However, most child sexual abuse cases are handled by individual states and will depend on state laws.

In Miami-Dade County, Florida, for example, sex offenders (or convicted abusers) have to be listed on a sex offender registry and they cannot live within 2,500 feet (762 m) of a school, daycare center, park, or playground, whereas in North Carolina, it's 1,000 feet (305 m). In Texas a person who is convicted for the second time of raping a child under fourteen can be put to death. If the offender is released from prison and registered with the sex offender registry, she or he may receive therapy to try to deter them from committing more crimes.

You can read more about your individual state laws at RAINN's state law database, https://apps.rainn.org/policy/.

Remember that every case is different, and only a team of lawyers, prosecutors, judges, and juries can decide exactly what will happen to an abuser.

If the perpetrator is a fellow student . . .

Unless the abuse is severe and on a criminal level, peer abuse is usually handled between the victim's family and the school.

Just like the case with Mr. Densch on page 116, a report will be made and an investigation will be launched. These reports are circulated to the administration, who can decide what to do with the perpetrator. The student may be punished for sexually abusive behaviors, placed in an anti-bullying program (especially for repeat offenses), or removed from general education and placed in a different track. Expulsion, transfers, and suspension are considered last resorts, since that student also has a right to the best education possible.

Remember, all of this should be outlined in your school's Title IX policy.

However, if the perpetrator has committed an aggravated assault against a peer, the student might be charged criminally. This might land in the juvenile justice system, leading to court or imprisonment. Yes, middle graders can be put in juvenile detention. Some states have a minimum of age ten, others as young as six.

If the perpetrator is a sibling or other young person outside of school . . .

Sibling abuse is actually more common than child abuse, and unfortunately, it's not always taken seriously. Sometimes, parents dismiss abuse as common sibling rivalry.

Once you tell a parent or trusted adult that your sibling is abusing you, however, they should intervene to set better boundaries and stop the behavior. If they don't succeed, the family should seek professional help. If the abuse is severe, the abused child might be removed from the home for safety. The abusive sibling could be sent to juvenile detention if the parents press charges or if the abusive sibling is caught by another adult.

If abusers are not prosecuted or convicted . . .

You are still entitled to file a civil suit—or sue—the abuser. Then a court will not determine whether the abuser is guilty of the crimes, but it may force the abuser to pay the victim for things such as emotional distress or assault and battery. Some states, including New York, will even allow you to wait and sue your abuser until you reach fifty-five years of age.

Expect nothing from the abuser.

In cases of potential misunderstanding, you might be able to get an apology or even some changes in a perpetrator's behavior. The case of Gianna and Mr. Densch on page 116 is a promising candidate for this kind of closure.

Childhood harassers might grow out of their behavior.

For example, someone who posts a "best butt" and "worst butt" list will probably not do such things as an adult, with the realization that it was a stupid and hurtful thing to do. This is part of natural maturing.

Serious young abusers will probably need a lot more intervention and care, but possibly they too can change. At the time of the abuse, they may not have the brain chemistry or tools to care about the damage they're doing to others. Not that this excuses bullying or abuse, of course. But kid abusers do have a better chance of becoming nonabusers later.

However, people, especially adults, who routinely abuse other people are usually damaged. They often lack empathy or remorse. They won't admit to wrongdoing. Once accused, they may start to attack a victim or act like victims themselves. They don't truly care about their victims—they use them. Once a victim reports abuse, the victim is no longer useful to an abuser, and so the abuser may say just about anything to get out of the situation.

In the case of seventeen-year-old Lauren Book (page 76), her abuser Waldina told law enforcement that she loved Lauren and never forced her to do anything (a lie). Waldina wrote Lauren love notes from prison that subtly demanded money, because Lauren's father was wealthy. When the letters got Waldina in trouble, she tried to have Lauren and her younger brother kidnapped for ransom from inside prison walls. Thankfully, she was unsuccessful. It could be argued that, after all those years of saying she loved Lauren, of torturing and raping her, that Waldina was secretly after her father's money all along.

Thankfully, most law enforcement officials see through

this type of behavior. Victims, however, may still be emotionally attached to their abusers on some level. They may hope for an apology, closure, or for a human connection. It is tremendously hurtful when abusers don't deliver on their promises, and unfortunately, most of the time, they don't. This is why it's so important to separate from an abuser, heal independently, and not expect anything positive from them. Comfort needs to come from professionals and the people who truly love you.

WHEN ADULTS FAIL

In an ideal world, adults do everything right. Parents believe their children. Teachers believe their students. Adults follow proper protocol and offer support to the victim. Perpetrators get what's coming to them, and maybe they even apologize. It's all wrapped up in a neat bow, just like in the movies.

But sometimes, adults can't see past their own beliefs or ignorance, and they can't offer support to abused children, not even their own.

Cultural Differences Some families, because of their cultures or religions, don't protect victims even within their own family. In these situations, there might be victim-blaming or a disinterest in involving authorities. For example, some deeply religious families are so concerned about their child's virginity status that they don't want to report a rape, or they become angry with the child victim.

An adult shouldn't react this way. This reaction doesn't help the victim's healing and well-being. Nothing is worse than shaming a victim who is already in crisis.

If you are in a family or culture with very strict victim-shaming viewpoints, you probably can't change their opinions. You may have to seek help outside of this community or at least not let it bother you—which is easier said than done.

CHANDRA'S STORY (TRUE)

For almost three years in their home in India, Chandra's uncle touched her inappropriately. He put his fingers inside her while she was sleeping, he peeped on her while she was in the shower, and he made her sit on his lap in a creepy way. He molested her regularly. It started when she was ten.

Three years into the abuse, she read about sexual abuse in the newspaper. It was the first time she'd ever heard of it. She worked up the nerve to tell her parents.

After hearing Chandra's story, her parents confronted her uncle and made sure the two didn't have contact again. However, her parents—particularly her father—wanted to keep the matter private. Her mother argued, but men always had the final say in their family.

Her uncle still got rights, respect, and dignity within the extended family as if nothing had ever happened. Chandra was angry with her parents for a long time.

It was taboo for Chandra to seek help, so she didn't get any help until many years later, when the lingering trauma started to affect her relationship with her husband.

It's hard to completely fault Chandra's parents. In their culture when this occurred, men had the final say, therapy was frowned upon, and sexual abuse wasn't discussed at all. If you're not from a culture like this, you can easily scoff, but for the sake of upholding family honor, Chandra's parents did what they felt they had to do. She probably couldn't have changed their minds.

If only Chandra had had resources other than the newspaper, such as another adult she could speak to, a hotline, or more books she could read on the subject.

Most of us have access to these things. No matter how stuck you may feel in your family, help is available.

Cults and Abusive Institutions It's very difficult if you are part of a small religious order, a cult, or in a system such as a juvenile detention or a boarding school where sexual abuse is rampant.

When children are isolated from the rest of the world, it's easy for predators to get away with sexual abuse, brainwashing, chronic victim-blaming, and isolating victims.

In a cult, a leader typically lures adults to an isolated place with some sort of holy promise, and children of those adults have to follow. Remember the description of grooming from page 55? It's a bit like that, only a leader is grooming a big group of victims instead of just one. A cult might enable the sexual abuse of children, or it might even be part of the rules. The Children of God and the Fundamentalist Church of Jesus Christ of Latter-day Saints, for example, were both at one time run by known pedophiles who abused many children and justified it with Bible scripture.

People tend to hear about cults because they're so extreme that they get a lot of press. However, acts of abuse in cults are pretty isolated incidents. Kids are vulnerable to sexual abuse in any institution, whether it's religious (the Vatican has a backlog of over two thousand sex abuse cases throughout the Catholic Church), or in prisons (some children are incarcerated alongside adults, where they are *highly* vulnerable to abuse), or even in schools (many New England private schools were recently exposed for decades of sexual abuse, along with very unethical cover-ups). Every church and school isn't like this, of course, but it's up to the people in charge to stay vigilant so that abuse doesn't become a problem. When the people in charge of an institution don't care, these kids are more vulnerable than anyone.

A major reason why institutional abuse is so common is because the children have been separated from their parents. It's a horrible report to read, but it was not surprising to learn that thousands of migrant children who are being detained at the US border have reported sexual abuse at the hands of staff and other minors. *Thousands, right now, in the United States.*

Fighting abuse from within these institutions as a child takes more bravery and insight than just about anything in this book, so reporting and getting help in these situations is not something we should expect from a kid. These scenarios are so extreme, and reporting might not be safe or possible. Escaping a cult and talking to the police is not easy, nor should that burden lie on the child. It *has* happened—a fifteen-year-old girl named Verity Carter escaped the Children of God cult after being abused since the age of four—but that's an exception, not the rule. In these institutional cases, adults need to step in to protect the children.

If a child has been freed from such a situation, he or she needs counseling right away.

When Justice Fails Sometimes justice works. Comedian Bill Cosby was convicted of drugging and raping women and sent to prison. Catholic priests around the world are being arrested for abusing children, and the church has even rolled out a few apologies. Singer R. Kelly is finally being brought to justice after years of allegations that he harmed teenage girls, though as of the writing of this book, his fate has yet to be sealed.

However, our justice system is also flawed, imperfect, and often completely unjust. In 2016 a judge sentenced Stanford University athlete Brock Turner to just six months in prison after he was convicted of raping an unconscious woman. After serving only three months, he was set free.

Then there's the terrible case of Amber Wyatt, which you can read about on page 86. Wyatt told law enforcement that she had been brutally raped by two soccer players. There was even physical evidence. However, the town protected the boys so fiercely that the investigation went nowhere. Worse, her schoolmates bullied her for accusing the boys.

There are many depressing cases like this, and they all point to different failures in the justice system and in our thinking.

A sex abuse case can go sideways in multiple ways. You are dealing with a broken system in these cases:

- A school cares more about its reputation and protecting

abusers than helping students.

- Incompetent or untrained people are put in charge of interrogating you, whether it's at school, a doctor's office, or a police station. (Training on handling child abuse victims is available for these people, but not everyone knows that.)
- You live in a small town where people protect abusers, such as the local high school football stars or other beloved characters.
- You get a judge, a jury, or an entire town that believes abuse victims deserve it, that abuse victims should just protect themselves, or that victims are lying.
- You live in a big town or city where your case sits at the bottom of a huge pile and gets less attention.
- Having money or connections is the only way to get justice.
- You or your caregivers have to push for an extremely long time to get anywhere with law enforcement or the school.

These problems are not everywhere. Some places take sex abuse charges very seriously and have a strong system in place. However, these types of problems are very common, and they need to be changed.

I hope that you and your loved ones never have to deal with any of these situations. If it makes you angry to read this, you're not alone. In chapter 6, we'll talk about how you can get involved and help change broken systems.

LEIDY & BARB'S STORY (TRUE)

You read about Leidy, Nadia, and Mikel on page 46. Here's what happened next.

The slut-shaming and bullying got so out of control that Leidy's mother, Barb, had to get involved. Barb went to the school to talk to the Title IX coordinator. Barb didn't know anything about this stuff—she just wanted the bullying to stop, and she had full faith that the school would intervene and help her daughter.

Barb ended up in Mr. Doneghy's office. He was an assistant principal, but Barb couldn't imagine a worse person for this particular job. He was gruff, old school, and didn't seem to have any sexual harassment training. He told Barb that "boys will be boys" and that "girls do the whole cyberbullying thing sometimes." Barb insisted that he do something about it—at least punish the bullies and put them in different classes from Leidy. She also knew there were anti-bullying classes available to students.

For weeks, Mr. Doneghy did nothing, according to Barb. Finally, Barb presented some of the bullies' slut-shaming notes. Then at least there was some physical evidence.

According to Barb, instead of sending the kids to anti-bullying training, Mr. Doneghy invited Mikel, Nadia, Nadia's complicit friends, and Leidy to sit in his office together. He told the bullies to apologize for the notes and their behavior. Leidy was extremely uncomfortable, and the students were obviously only apologizing because Mr. Doneghy was there.

After that, the bullying got worse. This time, the students were retaliating against Leidy for reporting them. Nadia remained the ringleader, and she and Leidy were still in the same class.

Barb continued to complain to Mr. Doneghy, but nothing changed, Barb said.

Barb escalated her report to the school district superintendent. The school principal, Ms. Porter, angrily called Barb. "Why would you call downtown?" Ms. Porter demanded. Barb told Ms. Porter what had been happening to her daughter. This was the first time they'd spoken.

Ms. Porter responded by subjecting the whole school to sexual harassment training in an assembly. During the training, Mikel stood up and said directly to Leidy for the whole school to hear: "I think this is all fake." Leidy reported this, which Barb said made the retaliation worse.

In a desperate act, Leidy took the law into her own hands. She begged Mikel to stop the bullying and the circulation of her suggestive photo. He agreed, but only under the condition that she give him $400. Over time, Barb said, Leidy stole cash from her mother's wallet and handed it to Mikel.

When Barb found out about this, she told the police and hired a lawyer. Blackmailing could be considered a very serious crime, but when Barb looked into it five days later, she said that the law enforcement, the school, and the lawyer had done nothing. They hadn't questioned Mikel, gone to his house, or anything else. The lawyer was very soft on the school, according to Barb, and thought that the sexual angle wasn't strong enough. He believed that since

Leidy was a student of color, their case would be stronger if they played up a racist angle.

Barb was growing suspicious that the officials and experts were protecting the school's reputation, which was the pride of the town. She speculated that this club mentality was why no action was taken. Barb never once heard anything about Nadia's or Mikel's parents or whether they had been informed of everything that was going on.

Leidy's confidence had all but disappeared. She was much quieter than she used to be and had lost her bubbly personality. Barb found her a trauma counselor who visits the house regularly.

Meanwhile, the bullying continued. A few boys cornered Leidy one day after school and groped her breasts. Leidy reported the incident to Ms. Porter, who was sympathetic, but said she couldn't do anything without corroborative witnesses, according to Barb.

One day, a very connected city superintendent named Gloria invited Barb out to lunch. Barb said that Gloria casually mentioned another school in town and dropped hints that Leidy might be very happy to be transferred there.

Barb responded that Leidy just wanted a good education and that she was entitled to one at her current school. But Barb knew that the pressure to transfer was on.

This story is gut-wrenching. On every level, the school system is allegedly failing Leidy, the law is failing her, and all of these failings pressured Leidy into foolishly taking the law into her own hands, with terrible results.

The school allegedly failed right from the get-go when Mr. Doneghy started by dismissing Leidy's claims. Even if he didn't think her claims were a big deal, he was required by law to report them.

Ms. Porter was allegedly angry with Barb for reporting the harassment to people with higher authority. This demonstrates that Ms. Porter cares more about herself and the school than for sexual harassment victims. She sees Barb as a nuisance, rather than seeing Nadia and Mikel as behaviorally disturbed kids who desperately need discipline and reeducation.

Leidy's lawyer, according to Barb, did not fight for Leidy's Title IX rights, and law enforcement did not launch a true investigation.

Gloria the superintendent allegedly ignored the sexual harassment issue. Instead, she was practically complicit in bullying Leidy by encouraging her to leave her school. Even if transferring to a new school might be best for Leidy, Gloria is not taking any responsibility for fixing the current school culture.

Leidy's civil rights may have been violated because of her school's inability to provide a comfortable educational setting without sexual or gender-based harassment, as well as physical abuse.

However, two things happened properly in this story. Leidy had a trusted adult, Barb. Barb always believed Leidy and used her own power as an adult and a parent to fight for Leidy and learn about school proceedings. Leidy also received counseling, which is crucial considering the nature of this abuse. Probably, Leidy would be completely lost otherwise.

As of this writing, Barb continues to fight for her daughter while weighing the options of transferring. She spearheaded a parent group in the school to help combat sexual harassment, but she is unsatisfied with the results so far. Other outlets that Barb might be able to pursue are hiring another lawyer to sue the school or involving the press.

It should never have gotten to this level.

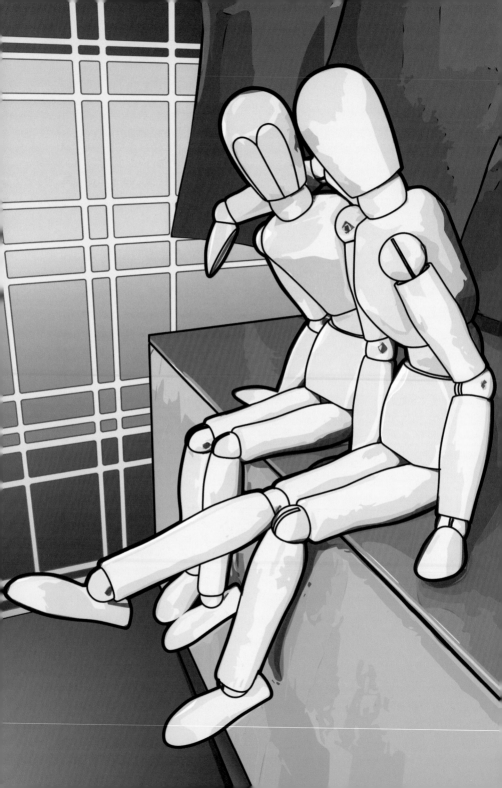

CHAPTER 5

BEING AN ALLY

An ally is a supporter of an abuse victim. Without allies, victims would probably never get the help they need. Being an ally is extremely important.

Anyone can be an ally, including a friend, a teacher, a parent, a stranger on a hotline, or even an anti-abuse protester on the street. You're already an ally because you're reading this book and educating yourself.

You don't have to be an expert to be an ally. You don't have to save the world, put yourself in unsafe situations, or make yourself crazy. You don't even have to know an abuse victim personally. Being an ally is something you carry with you at all times. It's a skill set and a way of life that you can use anytime. And you can teach others.

This chapter is all about the guiding principles of being an ally. There is no explicit sexual or violent content in this chapter, but the previous chapters can help give more context. As in chapter 4, I may refer to an ally as "you" to make everything easier to understand.

ACTIVE UPSTANDER VERSUS COMPLICIT BYSTANDER

If you see an abusive situation unfolding in front of you, you have two choices: be an active upstander or be a complicit bystander. An active upstander sees a situation and stands up for what's right. A complicit bystander allows or even encourages a situation to unfold.

You might be picturing somebody getting physically attacked, and then the upstander has to decide whether to bust out the big guns and fight the villain and save the day. Never say never, but that's usually reserved for the movies.

Here are some less glamorous but more practical examples of active upstander behavior:

Tell an adult when something bad has happened.

Call 911 if you witness a crime.

Teach a friend to stop slut-shaming or using victim-blaming language.

Notice when someone is uncomfortable, and check in with them by saying, "Hey, you okay?"

Notice that your friend or friends are making someone uncomfortable, and tell them to back off.

Don't engage in abusive behavior, and voice your disapproval when you see it. For example, if a friend shows you nude photos of a classmate, tell him that it's not right and don't look at the photo with your friend. Others will follow. (Also, tell the victim what happened, and tell an adult. The photo is technically illegal since it features a minor.)

Document an abuse incident you saw: the time, the place, and what happened. It might help the victim later.

Volunteer to be a witness for the victim in the principal's office, in the guidance counselor's office, or wherever the victim needs you.

Don't gossip about a sexual abuse incident. It's nobody's business but the victim's.

Document an incident with your phone *only if it helps the victim*, not to post on Snapchat without the victim's consent.

Listen to a victim.

If you see someone getting attacked on social

media, drop the victim a DM to say that you're there for them, and ask if they need anything.

Stand up to a bully, if it's safe.

Okay, sure, an active upstander can also come in and save the day and stop a terrible attack. But you're not Superman, and it's very important that you stay safe too.

A complicit bystander sees an incident and does not help the victim in any way. Sometimes, a complicit bystander might even encourage the incident. Here is some classic complicit bystander behavior:

Witnessing abuse and doing nothing about it before, during, or after.

Witnessing abuse and laughing.

Praising abusers for their behavior.

Gossiping about the incident or spreading the story around.

Sharing a post or picture that is harmful to the victim.

Taking a video of an incident to post on social media without the victim's consent.

Taking a video of an incident instead of helping in other ways. If a person is in physical danger and needs your help, put down the phone.

It's possible to be paralyzed and not know what to do in the moment, especially if an incident is a total surprise. We've all had times when we wished we'd done something differently or said something different in the moment, but we froze instead. However, you can always tell an adult later, help the victim afterward, or shut down malicious gossip. We are all responsible for being active upstanders.

Remember the golden rule of power dynamics from page 25: a person with more power in a dynamic should *always* protect and uplift someone who has less. In an abuse dynamic, bystanders have more power than a victim. Use it for good.

HOW TO TELL IF SOMEONE IS BEING ABUSED

It's rare that you can spot abuse on a victim. Even experts can't nail it down to a science.

Below is a list of potential signs that someone is being abused. However, be cautious. All of these may be signs of a different problem. Some of these things might just be natural signs of experimentation and growing up, or some might happen because a person has depression genes in the family (which is worth examination and treatment). Do not jump to conclusions. You won't know definitively if someone is being abused unless you witness it or somebody credible tells you about it.

Regular bruising and cuts

Sudden drastic changes in behavior

Self-injury, such as cutting or careless behavior

Problems sleeping

Becoming antisocial or withdrawn

Listless or secretive behavior

Uncharacteristic mood swings, such as anger, tears, or sadness

Not eating or eating more than usual

A sudden fear of being left alone with someone

Fear of being touched

Changes in quality of schoolwork or grades

Acting younger or engaging in younger behaviors or activities

Sudden, unexplained fears of certain places or people, such as all people with a particular feature or characteristic

Substance abuse

Delinquency

Persistent sex play with friends, toys, or pets

Frequent drawings that include sexual content

Severe anxiety, such as nightmares or clinging

Depression, which might include withdrawal, low self-esteem, thinking about or attempting suicide, or frequent crying

Unusual, persistent, or inappropriate questions about human sexuality

If you're involved in a victim's life after abuse, keep an eye on the victim. Abuse victims sometimes engage in self-destructive behavior, such as cutting, drinking, getting involved in bad relationships, acting out, or skipping class. Tell an adult if you notice something drastic or off. It's not tattling if you're helping them get better.

BELIEVING AND LISTENING

Abuse victims need people to believe them and to listen to them.

If a peer tells you he's been abused, he's trusting you. It probably took a lot of courage to speak up, and he chose you as a trustworthy, attentive, and kind ear. You might be shocked by what he says, but as an ally, you have a responsibility to believe and listen. Here's how:

Even if you're shocked or don't know what else to say, "I believe you" is a strong statement that can go a long way toward being a good ally. It's also very easy to say. If you say nothing else, say that.

Sometimes a victim just needs someone to listen, which means sitting there and hearing the story.

Don't butt in with your own personal stories or ideas or change the subject. Sometimes people do this when they're uncomfortable, but try to restrain yourself.

Refrain from having a very intense emotional reaction in front of the victim. It won't help if you get really upset or angry or start threatening

to kill the abuser. Try to remain calm, and save any intense reactions for when the victim isn't around. Having a reaction is normal, but in that moment, it's important to keep the focus on the victim and not fly off the handle.

It's okay to react in a less intense way or to say "I'm so sorry" and give hugs. It's okay to cry. You don't have to have some perfect script. Again, the victim mostly needs you to listen and believe.

Do not be incredulous or act as though you don't believe the victim. For example, don't say, "Did that *really happen?*" or "Are you exaggerating?" or "No way. He would *never* do that. He's *way* too nice." Just listen and keep those feelings to yourself. You could be doing a lot more damage than you think.

Do not blame the victim. Never tell victims that they should have defended themselves during the attack or ask questions like, "Why were you even with him in the first place?" or "I would never let someone do that to me" or "You were wearing a miniskirt, soooo . . . " Chances are, the victim is doing her fair share of self-shaming, and she doesn't need your help with that.

Do not judge the victim on her pain. Maybe you don't think the abuse was that big of a deal and you don't know why she's crying so much. Maybe the abuse happened a long time ago, so you don't know why she's still angry about it. Everyone deals with abuse trauma in different ways, and all of them are valid. Voicing those opinions may do damage, so keep those feelings to yourself.

You're going to feel uncomfortable in this situation. There is no doubt about that. These conversations are uncomfortable. It's up to you to decide if you can handle the discomfort and responsibility of hearing the victim, or if the victim's story is too upsetting or triggering for you. If you'd rather not take it on, you don't have to. But be extremely gentle. The victim is very vulnerable, and you don't want to make him afraid to speak up. You might say something like, "I love you very much and I believe you and I am so sorry about what happened to you. However, I am not personally in a good place to hear this. It's not you, and it's not because you shouldn't speak up. I think you should talk to (a teacher, your parent, a school counselor, or another friend). They might be more capable of listening than I am right now. When I am ready to hear it, I will tell you. In the meantime, is there another way I can help?"

RESPECTING BOUNDARIES

Respecting a victim's boundaries is a very important step for an ally. It's tough, because a good ally really wants to help, but you don't want to push. A victim needs space to heal.

Here are some tips for respecting a victim's boundaries:

Say something like, "I'm here to talk if you need me," but don't say it a million times or push someone to talk. She'll come to you if and when she's ready.

Remember your role. You're not the victim's therapist or parent, and you don't have to be. The victim should get that type of help and support from adults. Maybe you're the sister, the brother, the friend, or the cousin. Even if you're an ally, you're *still* the sister, the brother, the friend, or the cousin, and your role in the victim's life doesn't change much. It's not your job to diagnose the victim, to learn the ins and outs of the law, or to "save" anyone.

Victims usually need to try to resume normal life. While some things will inevitably change, you shouldn't treat a victim much differently than you used to. For example, keep inviting them to parties even if you don't think they'll come. Don't feel that you have to constantly talk about the abuse with them. Take their lead and act as naturally as you can.

A victim may not be ready to resume certain normal activities right away. Have patience and don't force it.

Don't overdo it with information. It's okay to gift

one book about sex abuse, but it's less okay to bombard a victim with *many* books, *many* links, or *many* similar stories. It may feel as if you're being helpful, but this might become overwhelming or triggering for the victim. You don't know what might hurt them, so slow down.

Don't assume that victims need you around, need lots of hugs, or need hot cocoa all day long. Sometimes they want to be left alone. If you're unsure, just ask, "Should I come over, or would you rather be alone?" Don't take it personally if they want some space. They are going through a lot, and they need to be able to say no to you without it being a big deal.

Under no circumstances should you try to take the victim's healing into your own hands. For example, do not confront the abuser or launch a campaign against him or her, no matter how angry you are. Do not plan a big social gathering for the victim unless she's involved in the planning. This could have disastrous effects.

Remember that the best thing you can do is listen and be there. You don't need to do a bunch of extra stuff.

RESPECTING PRIVACY

Respecting a victim's privacy can be difficult in the gossiping world of middle or high school. You talk to your friends all day, and here is a huge thing weighing on your mind.

However, respecting privacy is probably one of the most important things you can do as an ally (along with believing the victim).

Keeping a secret is different from respecting privacy. Allies should not keep secrets of sex abuse from adults or the authorities. Respecting a victim's privacy is about allowing someone to heal without fear of gossip.

Here are some tips:

Unless they tell you otherwise, assume that the victim doesn't want anyone to know outside of the authorities and caregivers involved.

Do not post anything on social media about it.

Do not vaguebook, or talk about it in vague terms, on social media. Even if people can't identify the victim, the victim might be triggered by your post.

If you need to talk about it, tell a guidance counselor or an adult caregiver you trust. This will help you get things off your chest in a way that doesn't harm the victim. Or call one of the confidential hotlines listed in the Additional Resources to talk to a professional.

Consequences of gossip are real. Remember, everything you say and write might affect the victim's case.

TELLING AN ADULT

Kids are not bound by mandatory reporting (see page 104). However, allies should always report abuse they've witnessed, heard about, or that they strongly suspect. The same rules of reporting apply to allies. Talk to a trusted adult, stick to the facts, don't expect things to move quickly, and exercise self-care.

KNOW YOUR LIMITS AND SET YOUR OWN BOUNDARIES

Yes, being an ally takes some sacrifice. It takes time, discomfort, and self-restraint. It's rewarding and important, but it isn't your entire life. Know your own limits so that you don't drive yourself nuts.

If you feel that the victim is asking too much of you (for example, if he wants to text you all day every day or if she wants you to sleep over every night), draw some boundaries. You can be a good ally without giving up your life. Your independent relationships with your school, your friends, and your family should all remain high priorities. You do not need to feel guilty.

You may be a comfort to the victim, but only real professional help and support will get a victim through this. If you take a day or two off from talking about the abuse, that isn't going to set off a crisis. You are responsible for being an ally, not for being a 24-7 caregiver, or even a 2-7 caregiver. It's up to you to set your limits.

If a victim is outright guilting you into taking care of him or if she's threatening that a crisis will happen if you don't show up, you are in an unhealthy relationship that needs to be reexamined. See chapter 1 on the definition of an unhealthy relationship.

BEING TRIGGERED

If you're deeply involved with a victim, being an ally can have an emotional effect on you. Even though the focus is usually on the victim's feelings, an ally's feelings are important too.

As you've learned, being uncomfortable is par for the course when you're an ally, but being triggered is different. You may hear the word *triggered* used as kind of a joke. However, in this book, the word is very important.

If you are triggered, it means that something is reminding you of something *very* negative in your own life. Maybe this thing in front of you puts you in a bad emotional place, makes you feel terrible, or dredges up memories that you don't want to remember.

If you have also experienced abuse, being an ally can be very triggering. It might remind you of something that has happened or is currently happening in your life.

You can feel triggered by seeing a movie or by reading a book that has intense content. (I've put content, or trigger, warnings throughout this book.) In the same way, sexual abuse allies can feel triggered when they hear a victim's stories, witness abuse, or take on the role of helper after abuse takes place. Sometimes we don't even notice we're being triggered. We just feel terrible.

But someone who has been through abuse makes a great ally. That person can understand the situation more than others.

However, you can't be a great ally until you've faced your own stuff and healed through counseling, which you can do by going through the steps of seeking help (see chapter 5). Being triggered every day without support can only hurt you further. Take care of yourself first.

If you feel badly triggered, tell the victim that you're not ready to be a certain kind of ally yet. Offer some other ways that you can help. Maybe you can't hear your friend's story of abuse or comfort him through his sadness, but you *can* pick up his school worksheets and other homework and bring them to his home.

PILAR'S STORY (FICTIONAL)

Pilar was doing better than ever at soccer practice. As the sweeper defense, she was owning the scrimmage and getting ball after ball away from the goal. Her mother, the assistant coach, watched proudly.

Toward the end of practice, parents started to show up to pick up their kids. Pilar's friend Inez's mom showed up with their new puppy, Pika. Pika was very cute and wild. Pilar had met him earlier at Inez's house, and she had fallen in love. But when Pika ran up to the soccer coach and jumped on him gleefully, Pilar got a sinking feeling. She suddenly felt very angry and upset, and she didn't want to scrimmage anymore. She let a couple of balls fly past her, and before practice was over, the opposing team scored two goals.

Afterward, on the car ride home, Pilar's mom asked her if anything was wrong.

"No," Pilar said. "I don't know."

Pilar felt angry and upset the whole ride home. When she opened the door to their apartment, she felt like something was missing.

Her dog, Stimpy, had died last year. He wasn't home to greet her. She started to cry. It was so weird. When Stimpy had died, she had been sad, but not like this. She'd entered her apartment hundreds of times since then and felt fine. He was just a dog, after all.

It seems that Pilar was triggered by seeing Pika jump on her soccer coach. Maybe it reminded her of Stimpy jumping on her, and her feelings about Stimpy finally came to the surface. She didn't really understand **why** she was upset, but she knew that she was.

Pilar hadn't mourned Stimpy when he'd died last year. She'd thought he was just a dog, and so she buried her feelings and didn't let herself feel bad at the time. Unfortunately, you can't just get rid of feelings. If you don't deal with them, they can hurt you in other ways, like the way this feeling hurt Pilar's soccer performance.

It's obvious that Stimpy **wasn't** just a dog to Pilar. He meant a lot to her, and she needs to heal and face her emotions before she can move on.

VICARIOUS TRAUMA

Vicarious trauma can happen to people who listen to victims' stories. Vicarious trauma would mean that you, the ally, feel trauma because you're experiencing a victim's painful, traumatic story in a deep and personal way.

Therapists get very rigorous training in vicarious trauma so that it does not affect them and their work. After all, therapists have to listen to patients' difficult stories all day. However, most of us don't have that training, and it can be very hard *not* to be very badly affected when a loved one is hurt. If any of the following things are happening, you might be experiencing vicarious trauma:

You dream about the victim's story.

You're losing sleep over the victim.

You're constantly worried that you're not doing enough to help.

You experience trauma symptoms such as anxiety, eating more or less than usual, depression, low self-image, self-mutilation, or substance abuse.

You're not taking care of your own life because you're too busy focusing on the victim.

If you are experiencing any of these as an ally, you don't have to handle it alone or pretend to be stronger than you are. Talk to your caregiver or counselor about getting professional help.

These experiences may not be caused by vicarious trauma, but they're definitely symptoms worth noting.

HALLEY'S STORY (TRUE)

A mom named Halley—that's me—was writing a book about sexual abuse for middle graders. She put out a call to friends, acquaintances, and people with middle-grade kids. She asked if they wanted to share their own true stories. She thought she would have a hard time getting people to respond. Even though she was changing all their names, this stuff is so deeply personal and difficult to talk about. It seemed like too much to ask.

Halley was wrong. So many people responded that it

was actually overwhelming. People from all parts of her life wanted the book to help kids around the world.

Her friend Kaye (not her real name) was one of the first people who responded. She and Halley hadn't talked in a while, and it was good to catch up on the phone.

First, they talked about normal stuff: work, family, and life. Then Kaye asked Halley, "How do you feel, listening to all these stories?"

Halley had been a journalist and interviewer for a long time. She had heard so many horrible things in her career that she had assumed she would be fine.

She responded, "I'm good. It's hard, but hearing these things is motivating me to write the book." The truth was, Halley hadn't even thought about her own part in the conversation. She was just relieved that people wanted to talk to her.

Without further ado, Kaye told Halley her story. You can read it again on page 66, but—huge content warning—it's very disturbing.

Halley was absolutely floored. What her friend had gone through sounded like something out of a movie. It was so horrible, so terrifying—Kaye could have been killed, and she'd held that trauma with her for so long. During all of those times that Halley and Kaye had hung out, Kaye had been carrying this.

Halley played it cool on the phone, but when they hung up, she felt as though the wind had been knocked out of her.

She had trouble sleeping. She felt angry. She wanted to track down the guy who'd hurt Kaye and choke him to death. She was consumed by thoughts of other girls he must have hurt.

Halley had gone through her own sexual abuse in her life. She had been attacked by a friend in her sleep. Before then, a charming man who was much older had groomed her, escalated abusive behavior over years, and had raped her a number of times. In middle school, a boy had coerced her into a sexual act, then told the entire school that she was a slut. (She only recently recognized that it was coercion, and that she wasn't, in fact, a slut, whatever that word means.)

She had been talking about these incidents in therapy for many years, and while you can never heal 100 percent, Halley had done a lot of work on herself. She knew that writing this book might trigger these bad memories or that it might cause vicarious trauma. (Kaye's story is scary enough to traumatize anyone, with or without a history.) Halley knew she had to write it anyway. Being an ally and writing the book was way too important for her and for kids across the globe. But she knew she had to take care of herself too.

She told her therapist about Kaye's story. She did not say Kaye's real name, and the therapist legally cannot tell anyone else, so Halley knew it was okay. She told the therapist about sleeping issues she'd been having and about feeling angry. She had to be honest. It wasn't just because of Kaye's story. It was because of *all* the stories and research. It was so much to take on.

The therapist, let's call her Pat, said she was glad that Halley was concerned about her own mental well-being. Pat would have been *really* worried if Halley had been churning through the book unaffected, with absolutely no issues whatsoever. That would mean that Halley was burying a lot. As we've learned in this book, burying things can only make them worse.

Halley and her therapist devised a plan to talk about the book during their sessions, so Halley wouldn't be carrying all the weight on her own. Halley decided she would take frequent breaks from writing the book or skip to less triggering chapters if anything was feeling too heavy. Halley also did yoga every day, which was a great way to clear her mind and feel centered. She now has more tools to handle the mental load of writing this book. And look, it's almost done!

By being an ally and writing this book, Halley—again, that's me!—has put herself at risk of being triggered about her own abuse and also at risk of vicarious trauma. She knew the risks going in but was willing to take them. She had already done a lot of therapy and had faced her own stuff for years. So she felt prepared to be an ally to Kaye.

But of course, stuff happens. Kaye's story was more disturbing than Halley was prepared for, and it both triggered her and created some vicarious trauma. She realized that the whole book had been affecting her, and she needed to face these things head-on so the book wouldn't negatively affect her life.

Thankfully, Halley has a therapist and tools to deal with it. She took positive steps so that she could continue to be an ally. She's so proud of herself, apparently, that she decided to put this story in the book.

The lesson here is that nobody is immune to vicarious trauma, and that allies and listeners need to take care of themselves while they take care of others.

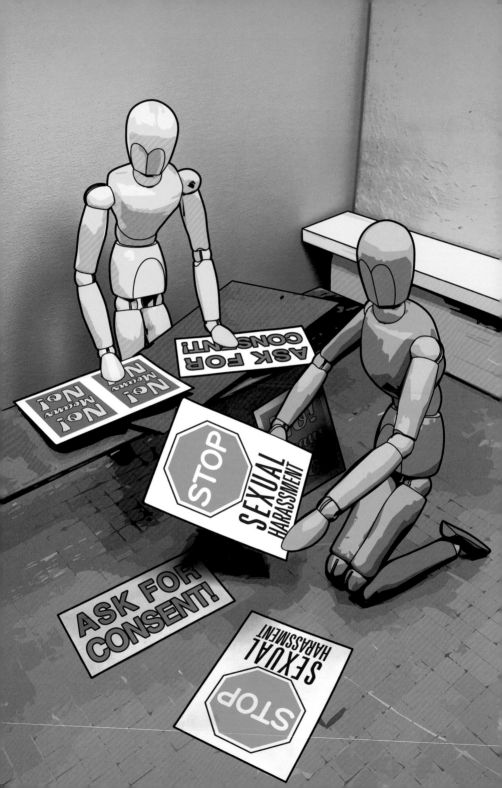

CHAPTER 6

TAKING ACTION

Content warning: The last section of this chapter contains disturbing violent and sexual content.

#MeToo starts with the things we do for ourselves and for other people in our lives. Until this chapter, this book has been all about individual incidents: what we do if something happens to us or to someone we know.

However, #MeToo is bigger than that. It's also about helping people we don't know. It's about raising awareness throughout schools, towns, and the world. It's about making things better for the kids who are younger than you, and it's about leaving the world a better place.

If you've read the book up to this point, you know that many abuse issues need to be fixed, such as the justice system, victim-blaming, or fear of reporting. You may not be able to change everything on your own. But you—yes, *you*—have the power to change the culture within your school and the world.

In this chapter, we'll talk about #MeToo activism. We'll go over situations where you may feel inclined to be a part of something bigger, as well as what steps you can take to fight for the cause, whether it's in your school or across the globe.

FIGHTING HARASSMENT IN YOUR SCHOOL

You are in school for about six hours a day. That's more than one thousand hours a year. That's a lot of hours—even more if you count extracurricular activities! If you're going to spend so much of your young life in one place, your school environment had better be comfortable and free of harassment. You are legally entitled to that.

If there is a sexual harassment problem in your school, report it. If you don't feel like reporting is enough and you want to do more, engaging in activism might be next.

AISHA'S STORY (TRUE)

Aisha and her classmates were playing badminton in gym class. Suddenly, she felt a hard thump on her behind.

Startled, she turned and saw that Marcus was running away, laughing, with a racket in his hand. Marcus had done stuff like that to other girls before, but never to Aisha. She was angry.

Aisha told the school guidance counselor, Ms. Pritchard, who said to Aisha, "Yes, we've had those issues with

Marcus. I don't think he's going to change."

Aisha found this reaction strange, since she thought Ms. Pritchard might have the authority to do something about it. Ms. Pritchard did talk to Marcus, who apologized to Aisha the next day. But the day after that, Marcus was up to the same tricks with different girls.

Aisha started to notice other stuff going on in her school. Her friend Imani had recently told her that a boy had shoved his hand in her shirt. When Imani went to Ms. Pritchard, nothing changed. Same when Nia said a different boy had slapped her butt.

The boys seemed to be getting bolder. Things would happen, and nobody would do anything. Gym class was getting *really* uncomfortable, since there was a higher chance of physical contact. Aisha realized that teachers talked about cyberbullying in school, but they never talked about sexual harassment or how to fight it. Health class was mostly about diet and fitness.

Aisha was angry, but she didn't know what to do. She felt that she was the only one in her school who cared at all and that the boys would just keep doing anything they could get away with.

Ms. Pritchard is not following protocol or helping Aisha or her friends. It is Ms. Pritchard's responsibility to work toward changing Marcus's behavior and to make sure that the girls in gym class—and every class—are safe from harassment. By not doing anything, the school is violating

Title IX, and the administration may be subject to legal action. (See pages 62 and 109 for more on this.)

While adults are the ones who are truly responsible, Aisha could channel her anger and powerless feelings into activism. Clearly, the school has a problem, and she is experiencing it firsthand.

Here are some steps to being an activist in your school:

Step 1. Identify the problems. Take a minute to write down the issues in your school. Try to stick to the facts as much as you can. For example, your concerns of "Nobody cares" or "The boys are always harassing us" will sound more accurate and will be taken more seriously if you write out: "There has been no decisive action from the administration" or "At least five boys have repeatedly harassed my friends and me by calling us inappropriate names and grabbing us" or "There is a culture of harassment in the school that makes kids feel uncomfortable in class."

If Aisha wanted to become an activist against sexual harassment in her school, she could start by identifying the problems.

Some boys are routinely engaging in inappropriate behavior, such as slapping girls on the behind or sticking their hands in girls' shirts.

These boys are not facing any consequences for this behavior, so it's getting worse.

The adults in the school are not acting.

There is no sexual harassment education in place.

Girls are feeling uncomfortable at school.

Step 2. Use those problems to create a clear vision for your goals.

It's very easy for causes to get overly complicated and muddy once they get moving. The problems that you outline in step 1 should serve as a guiding light to keep you focused. If Aisha wants her precise problems to get fixed in the school, she needs to stay on message. If we review the problems from the previous step, we can deduce that she is fighting for the following demands:

- People need to keep their hands to themselves.
- Consequences are needed for students who sexually harass others in school.
- Adults must be held accountable to respect Title IX and follow protocol.
- Sexual harassment education should be taught in school.
- School should be a comfortable place for girls.

Aisha might expand that last point to include other genders too. She wants all kids to be included in her movement. That small point—changing "girls" to "all students"—will not mess with her vision or the next actions she'll have to take. It's important to be open to some changes, since every movement may need some tweaking.

However, let's say Aisha starts talking to her friends about this issue, and they bring other complaints to the table. The girls' basketball team doesn't get as much money as the boys' team. The achievement gap between black and white students is at an all-time high. The cafeteria is too expensive for lower-income kids.

It's hard to leave any of these off the list, because they are all extremely important issues that need to be addressed. In a perfect world, one movement would solve every inequity. However, movements are more likely to make change if they are focused and unified behind a simple message or set of messages, and these new concerns have nothing to do with sexual harassment in the school.

Step 3. Review some actions you can take. You can do all kinds of things to fight harassment in your school. Below are a few ideas, starting from the smallest commitment and building to the largest. If you're aiming for the gold star at the end of this list, start small and work your way up.

Research. Research may not be the most glamorous step in activism, but it is one of the most important. Before she leaps into action, Aisha should find out her school's Title IX policy by talking to school officials. She could ask other students questions about their personal experiences with sexual harassment (under strict anonymity). She could ask friends in other schools what their experiences have been. If a formal investigation is ever conducted, Aisha might have to stop her reporting activities, but for now, she's the only one doing anything about the issue.

Write a letter to the higher-ups. Aisha could write a well-crafted letter to her school's superintendent, outlining the problems she's observed and demanding change. Aisha can demand that the school counselor be held accountable for sexual harassment consequences.

Put up messages around school. With the school's permission, Aisha can put up sexual harassment awareness posters at school. She could make her own or find inspiration from online examples.

Make art. Aisha could create activist art about sexual harassment. Art has been used for activism since the dawn of time. Depending on Aisha's talents, she might consider channeling her anger into writing, drawing, performance art, dance, video art, or music, and sharing it as widely as she can.

Start a petition. Aisha could start a petition to ask for sexual harassment education in her school and get as many

student and parent signatures as possible. She could then turn it in to the principal or superintendent.

Attend board meetings. School board meetings are run by a group of adults who make decisions about your school. These meetings, while boring, can be a great place to learn about school policy decision-making. Usually, anyone, including kids, can speak at the end of meetings. Aisha could prepare a well-written speech about the problems she has been facing, as listed in step 1. If she doesn't get the results she wants, she can keep going, again and again. This is an effective and immediate way to push change.

Write a proposal to the school. Aisha could put together a proposal for a sexual harassment awareness week. Some ideas in the proposal could include the following:

- putting up posters around the school
- a special assembly
- special guest speakers
- a required block of hands-on sexual harassment education for all students

Start an online group. Aisha could start an anti-sexual harassment group on social media for her classmates. She might want to have an adult adviser involved, such as a teacher, because this group may require a lot of moderation to keep victims safe and to keep bullies out. Eventually, this could grow into a website and an online community.

Start an after-school club. Aisha could talk to her school's administration about starting an after-school group, such as a sexual harassment awareness club, in which students can get together on a weekly basis to discuss anti-sexual harassment actions and encourage empowerment and speaking out. A teacher-adviser will be useful here, and it might be required if the club is affiliated with the school.

Involve the press. Aisha can send the petitions, her letter, and everything she's been working on to the press in her area. She should discuss this with a trusted adult first, to make sure she isn't jeopardizing any ongoing investigations or court cases. See step 4 on getting adult cohorts on your team to help you out.

Arrange a walkout or march. If change doesn't happen, Aisha can use her resources to organize a march or a school walkout.

Remember, this is just the idea phase. It takes a lot of work and organization to make some of these things happen. For example, it's very hard to race toward a march or school walkout without tons of help, preparation, and knowledge of your school's (and local police) policies. Every school is different, and it's easy for demonstrations to turn into chaos, and for your message to get lost.

By the time you're ready to organize a march or a school walkout, you'll have gathered plenty of resources and friends, and you'll know what it takes to make it happen successfully, with adult help. For more resources about organizing protests, turn to page 182.

Step 4. Collect your amazing team. Aisha is brilliant, no doubt about it. But it's going to take more than one student to make real and lasting change. That means she'll need some classmates, as well as adults, on board. So, how does she get them on board?

The more prepared she is with a plan, the better her odds

of collecting real cohorts. Anyone can tell Aisha that they're into her cause on an emotional level, but she's collecting *real* partners in activism, not fair-weather ones.

Here are some steps Aisha could take to collect a good team:

Approach with a plan. She could talk to a classmate or adult when they have free time. She would first tell them the problems collected in activism step 1, followed by the actions she plans to take from step 2. This approach is better than general questions like, "Do you hate sexual harassment?"

Pick good classmates. When it comes to approaching other kids, friends are a good place to start. Then Aisha might try kids who are already politically involved, such as student council representatives at her school. Not only should these kids listen to Aisha, but they have connections within the school to make things happen.

Pick even better adults. Adults are great to have on your side, whether they're parents, teachers, coaches, or administrators. Aisha should choose trusted (and connected!) adults and talk to them about her plans. She should ask for advice and learn from them.

Delegate. Aisha can't possibly do everything on her own. Not only does she not have time, but she doesn't have every skill on the planet. If her plan is to write a petition and she doesn't consider herself an amazing writer, for example, she might want to enlist some people who *are* great writers, as well as an adult proofreader. Or, if she's making a poster and she knows an outstanding illustrator, she can enlist that person to help if they want to. Some people are great at social media, public speaking, or music production. If Aisha doesn't want to be the leader, maybe she can get someone else to lead while Aisha handles organizing behind the scenes. In the end, a movement is usually better if people are playing to their strengths. Everyone will have more fun too.

Step 5. Fundraise for your cause.
If your cause has gotten to where you require funds, go to page 178 for suggestions.

If you are officially established with a good track record, your group or cause may be able to apply for grants, which are funds dedicated to worthy causes.

One place to start might be America's Promise Alliance, which periodically offers grant opportunities for youth who want to make a difference in their community. See https://www.americaspromise.org/. Or you could check out Youth Service America (YSA), which offers grants to kids for heroic initiatives, at https://ysa.org/grants/.

Better yet, get your cause sponsored by your school. Then school officials can apply for countless national, state, and local grants.

Step 6. Expect backlash.
In the social media age, backlash can come fast and hard, and it can get very ugly.

Emma González, a survivor of the 2018 Parkland, Florida, school shooting, was and continues to be a very outspoken activist on gun control. Her viral speech "We Call BS," aimed at politicians who support the National Rifle Association, was extremely powerful and moving for many people. For others, however, the speech provoked anger and even hatred. Right-wing media outlets made fun of her short hair. A Maine legislative candidate called her a "skinhead lesbian." Fake videos and conspiracy theories were spread around. A congressional representative used González's Cuban heritage to belittle her cause.

This was a very high-profile situation, but if you had asked most adults five years ago, we never would have thought that anyone—especially grown-ups and congressional representatives—would *ever* attack a high school student who had just been a victim of a violent, murderous attack. Even if they disagreed with her politics, what kind of an immature monster would *do* that?

Unfortunately, we would have been wrong. People will say anything to get a rise out of people and to hurt them.

More likely than crazed adults, you—or Aisha—would face internet trolling from fellow students, peers, or anonymous bored kids. It's impossible to truly prepare for an attack on your character, and it takes a lot of strength, focus, and support to ignore the haters and keep going. Here are some tidbits of advice:

Never engage with trolls. Imagine that trolls are like cars, and your anger toward them is like gas in their tank. If you do not engage, if you do not show them how their trolling affects you, they will eventually run out of gas.

Look away from the comments section. Seriously.

Keep your grace. If you get backlash from parents, students, teachers, the board of education, news outlets, or other people in your community, remember that this is the start of a very important dialogue. Keep your poise and keep your problems from step 1 clear in your mind. You have the truth on your side. Don't ever stoop to their level.

Backlash can be newsworthy. If you're interested in

involving the media, journalists *love* covering angry communities that try to suppress progress and justice.

Lean on your support system. Talk to your friends, family, and counselor about any cyberbullying. If you feel your safety is being threatened, your family may want to involve law enforcement.

Backlash means your movement is working. If you're getting backlash, it means that your movement has gotten somewhere. It has ruffled some feathers. For his civil rights activism, Martin Luther King Jr. got more backlash than anyone should have to bear. Of course, he's a tough act to follow, but remember that he wasn't a hero to everyone.

Step 7. Stick it out.

The world has a very short attention span. Massive media companies spend millions of dollars trying to get advertisements to stick in customers' heads, so it's pretty hard for one action to make a lasting impact on people in your school. It's going to take a lot of creativity and energy. If you feel the impact of your movement is flagging or if people are starting to lose interest before you've made a difference, that doesn't mean *you* have to lose interest or that it's all for nothing. It just means that the movement needs new life and energy. New poster designs, for example. New art. New cohorts. New identified problems and new goals. People *want* to feel energized and excited about something. Give the people what they want.

Step 8. However, don't lose your mind, prioritize.

If activism is taking over your whole life and all of your time, step back, take breaks, and handle your business.

You have your whole life ahead of you to make change, and you're of no use to anyone if you're beat down and worn out. #MeToo needs you strong, healthy, and educated, so don't slack on homework, sleep, or sanity for the sake of the cause.

Stepping back is not easy if you're passionate about something. Once you get started, it can feel as though you're never doing enough. The best way to approach activism is to start with smaller goals, such as changing one Title IX policy in your school or educating students on mandatory reporting. Smaller goals can actually be achieved, and they can make you feel much more accomplished. If you set out to "eradicate sexual harassment forever," then you will never be happy with your work.

FIGHTING HARASSMENT BEYOND YOUR SCHOOL

School is a great place for change. You know the lay of the land, the problems are very clear because you're seeing them firsthand, and it's easy to take the lead on a project. But #MeToo is big, and there's plenty of work to be done outside of your school's walls.

I wish I could say, "Just join the movement!" However, #MeToo is a little more complicated than that. The movement's founder Tarana Burke runs an organization called Girls for Gender Equity, which manages an excellent resource site for survivors and advocates at https://metoomvmt.org/.

However, #MeToo definitely took on a life of its own.

For example, the ME TOO Congress Act of 2017 would help White House workers submit sexual harassment claims more easily. Military hashtag #MeTooMilitary was created for members of the armed forces, and #MeTooSTEM was intended to protect victims in STEM professions. All of these causes cropped up completely separate from one another. Burke does not run those hashtags. #MeToo basically became a guiding principle that anyone can use to fuel change.

So, unless you're a very lucky person who gets to work directly with Burke, joining the movement beyond your school probably means linking up to a specific cause that deals with sexual abuse, consent, harassment, victim support, or anything else discussed in this book, but you can't just join the original #MeToo group.

Luckily, there are countless ways to get involved. Here's how to get started:

Pick a Cause Choosing a cause is a very important step. You need to find something that drives you so much that you're willing to endure the hard work and the occasional fatigue of fighting for it.

If you don't have something in mind already, this phase will take time and research. You may choose a general organization to support, a general organization you *don't* want to support (by boycotting, for instance), a current court case that means a lot to you, an unjust law, or a particular person or group of people who have been mistreated. All of these are specific causes of the #MeToo movement. The next part of this section outlines a few ideas for finding a cause.

Check out your local family or child crisis center. These organizations are dedicated to providing aid to children after a traumatic event. This kind of group is also sometimes called a **rape crisis center**. Some have teen volunteers.

Other local causes. You may be able to find local causes by searching a crisis center's newsletters, by scouring your town hall website, or exploring the library's community announcements. Depending on where you live, you might be able to find a local action calendar online. A lot of actions pick up steam on social media, so follow some local institutions that interest you. Follow and subscribe to local media outlets.

State organizations. Each state has accredited (which basically means legitimate) nonprofits that seek help and donations. You can find those, as well as state government agencies, at https://www.childwelfare.gov/organizations/.

National anti-sex abuse nonprofits. The following are a handful of accredited national nonprofits that usually welcome involvement and donations.

The Child Molestation Research & Prevention Institute (CMRPI), https://childmolestationprevention.org/, conducts research to prevent child sexual abuse and provides resources to everyone from agencies to families.

Darkness to Light, https://www.d2l.org/, provides training for adults throughout the country on how to handle incidents of child sexual abuse and trauma. (It's a great resource to show your parents or caregivers!)

Enough Is Enough, https://enough.org/, is a nonprofit dedicated to making the internet safe for children. This group has been on the forefront of fighting child pornography, child stalking, and sexual predation.

Kidpower, https://www.kidpower.org/, is a great anti-bullying organization that trains and empowers kids as well as adults. Preventing sexual abuse is part of their expansive programming.

Rape, Abuse & Incest National Network (RAINN), https://www.rainn.org/, is the largest national sexual violence nonprofit. They operate the National Sexual Assault Hotline, as well as a wide range of resources for victims and policy advocacy (fighting for better laws and enforcement).

Rights4Girls, https://rights4girls.org/, fights for girls' rights, including help for survivors of "child prostitution" and trafficking. I use quotes around child prostitute, because there is no such thing as a child prostitute, only child victims. Children cannot consent to prostitution.

Stop It Now!, https://stopitnow.org/, provides a helpline, prevention education, and policy advocacy.

Stop Sexual Assault in Schools (SSAIS), https://stopsexual assaultinschools.org/, is all about improving school policies, educating students and parents on their rights, and preventing assault in K–12 schools.

Stop the Silence, https://stopthesilence.org/, raises awareness about child sexual abuse through educational information, survivor groups, and healing resources. The group also holds races, walks, and events in local communities, so you could even bring Stop the Silence to your town.

You can find more national organizations at www.childwelfare.gov/organizations.

Find a specific current event or national cause. Is there a sexual harassment law that you don't agree with being debated in your town council? Did a judge make a sex abuse case decision that made you upset? Is there a #MeToo protest going on all around the world? These would be great causes to join. They're harder to seek out, though. Usually, they come to you.

Make sure it's legitimate. A *lot* of stuff is on the internet, including some scams, or just unofficial groups with unclear goals. Some of this is a waste of your time. Maybe a group of teenagers posted a Facebook invite about a flash mob, and it turns out to be chaotic and disorganized. Or you may think you're helping fight sexual abuse in a protest, but you're actually promoting a political candidate. Worst case, a false cause can create untold damage. The anti-vaccine movement started based entirely on false science that was debunked, and yet the movement only grew. As a result, small children are contracting diseases we all thought were eradicated.

If you want to make sure that a cause is legitimate, only work with official nonprofits, also called 501(c)(3) and charity organizations. You should be able to check a group's official status on the Internal Revenue Service website at https://www.irs.gov/charities-and-nonprofits. If you're linking up with a less official cause, such as a local protest against a law that's only advertised on social media, see if any official institutions are involved. Make sure only real people are signed up to go, not suspicious bots, and make sure a parent or caregiver comes with you. Don't give money to a cause unless it's an accredited nonprofit.

WAYS TO TAKE ACTION FOR YOUR CAUSE

1. Raise Money Raising money for a cause is a fantastic way to help. Sex abuse nonprofits and causes can almost always use more funding. And one benefit to raising money as opposed to other actions on this list is that you can live far away from the organization and still donate, even if you can't volunteer there. The options are vast.

Go the traditional route. Bake sales, craft sales, T-shirt sales (originally designed shirts with logos? Pretty cool!), book sales, raffles, or car washes—you probably know the drill. These are standard fundraising options, and the proceeds go to the cause of your choosing.

Start an online crowdsourcing campaign. You can start the campaign on Facebook, Indiegogo, Kickstarter, GoFundMe, or your own website. It's best if you have a specific goal or deadline in mind to motivate people to give. For example, Sexual Assault Awareness Month is in April. Maybe the fundraising campaign can be active from April 1 through April 30, and you have a goal of $5,000. (This number and time frame will change depending on your circumstances.) Spread the word through social media, at board meetings, or through school announcements.

Ask people to donate money to the cause in lieu of your birthday gifts. It takes serious dedication to give up a new PlayStation and all those Amazon gift cards, but this is a fabulous opportunity to send a message. It's such an amazing, bold, and selfless act that everyone will be sure to notice, which will help spread the word. Your friends may even copy you! Also, a birthday party is a great time to talk to friends and their parents about the causes that matter to you. They *have* to listen to you on your birthday. But keep in mind that giving up your presents can be rough. Don't force yourself to do it if it will only make you miserable.

Host a fundraising event. Putting on an event—a dance, a race, a haunted house, or a pool party—can be a great way to raise funds if you charge an entry fee. This can take a lot of planning, though, and it requires initial funding to cover a space, snacks, insurance, and so on. Adult involvement is a must. Even better if you can get an organization, nonprofit, or your school to help you directly.

Run a drive. A food, clothing, or coat drive can be a wonderful way to get goods to the people who need them. Kids who are abused are sometimes placed in homes and institutions, and they may be in need of these items. You might be able to put a bin in your school lobby and encourage kids to bring items from home. But it might be difficult to make sure these items go specifically to sexual abuse victims. If you run a drive,

you may need to broaden the cause to include all homeless or neglected children or adults.

Once you have an idea, remember to do the following:

Ask the organization or cause first. Most of the time, abuse nonprofit agencies are happy to receive money and goods. But you never know. An agency may be defunct, out of business, can't accept donations, or need to receive money and goods in a very specific way. You should know these things before you fundraise. They may even be able to help by sending you materials, giving you pointers, giving you a shout-out on their social media pages, or even helping you out in a hands-on way.

Get help from connected people. Talk to your student council representatives, school board members, and involved parents about your cause, and ask them for help. They may be able to spread the word through school announcements or have great advice or resources for fundraising.

Let the media know. Local media might be able to publicize your fundraiser as a featured article, a brief listing, or even a video or podcast spot.

Be very clear with donors. Be *very* explicit in your language with donors about where their money is going, and be prepared to confidently answer questions about the organization or cause that will receive the funds.

Be creative. You might get a good crowd with a standard fundraiser, but if you want to go bigger, or even go viral, you need to get creative. Enlist your amazing team (see page 169). Maybe you can put on a play, host a gaming tournament, or challenge people to do something crazy (yet safe and legal) on their phones with your cause's hashtag.

The more original the idea, the better. And the media loves it when someone so young takes initiative.

2. Protests, Boycotts, and Sit-Ins You probably know what all of these things are. A protest is a gathering, usually outside, where everyone might be holding signs, chanting, and singing for a cause. A boycott is when a large group of people refuses to buy or attend something out of protest. For example, activists debated whether to boycott Harvey Weinstein's movies after all the allegations came out. Sit-ins happen when protesters occupy a space and refuse to leave until their demands are met.

Participating in a protest, a boycott, or a sit-in can be one of the most gratifying experiences on this list. You get to feel like part of a community and energized by the movement around you. They are also great ways to attract media attention. That said, protests and sit-ins can be dangerous sometimes, so bring a caregiver and a buddy, and make sure that you're aligning with a legitimate cause.

3. Social Media Movements The #MeToo movement is predominantly online, and so are many other national movements. If you want to take a social media movement to the next level, you can spread a hashtag yourself or even try to start one (not many hashtag movements take off, though). You could also make a video, meme, podcast, blog, or original website that will grab an audience's attention. Drawing the attention of everyone in the country is not easy, however, unless you already have a huge following. If you have an idea to start or contribute to a social media movement, definitely run it by your caregiver and a few trusted adults before posting it for the world to see. That's a safety measure as well as a creative one.

4. Volunteer Work Hands-on volunteer opportunities for anti-sex abuse causes are very limited until you reach high school or college. Every city and town has different resources and opportunities, but due to the sensitive nature of the work at these organizations, most of them have volunteer age minimums.

Here are some opportunities for the future:

Family or child crisis center work. Many family or child crisis centers need volunteers in playrooms, on hotlines, or for office work.

Hotlines. You can train to be an operator at a confidential sex abuse or rape crisis hotline. This means you'd take calls from victims and help them get to the next step.

Political campaigns. If there's a candidate or a cause you strongly believe in, you can volunteer to work on a campaign. This might mean conducting polls, stuffing envelopes, setting up events, calling people, or any number of things. It doesn't sound as glamorous as protesting on the streets, but it's extremely important.

FIGHTING SEXUAL ABUSE ON AN INTERNATIONAL LEVEL

Content warning: This section contains very disturbing violent and sexual content. In some ways, this might be the most devastating section of this book.

Internationally, tales of sexual abuse in some countries are alarming and difficult to think about. Some countries have terrible human rights records, or they have been devastated by conflict and war, and therefore sex abuse, violence, and trafficking has been able to spread in a systematic way. That means sexual abuse isn't something that unfolds behind closed doors or in a courtroom. It means that it's happening at the hands of the government, the police, an army, tourists, or as part of the everyday culture with very few consequences.

As of the writing of this book, Pakistan, Egypt, and Mozambique are the worst countries in the world to be a child, according to a recent study, due to rampant sexual abuse and exploitation. The United States is ranked fifth in child safety, behind Australia, Canada, Sweden, and the UK, which is number one.

Of course, it's not a competition. Sexual violence against children is happening *absolutely everywhere.* One in twenty children in the UK has been abused, and that's supposedly the safest country.

We are seeing something unfolding in the United States right now that we never could have imagined. Thousands of children who have been detained at the US border have reported being sexually abused over the past four years. Many of these children haven't seen their parents in a long time. It may not sound like the United States we live in, but it is.

The whole world needs to improve.

For countries and groups in crisis like this, the #MeToo movement we know doesn't apply. Most of this book doesn't apply, either. In the scheme of the entire world, the #MeToo movement comes from a place of privilege. Some countries don't have basic gender rights (for example, very few girls can even go to school in South Sudan), or they have a legal system that's too corrupt to see any justice (as in Afghanistan), or poverty is so high that girls don't have a choice other than selling their bodies for food (the case for many girls in Mozambique). Teenage girls in Vietnam are regularly kidnapped and sold into sexual slavery in China, never to return to their families. Over two hundred million girls, mostly in Africa, the Middle East, and Asia have been subjected to female genital mutilation, which is the surgical removal of the clitoris to control girls' sexualities. The procedure can lead to serious physical, psychological, and sexual problems for the rest of their lives.

You can't tell these kids to speak up for themselves, to be empowered in the classroom, or to stand up against sexual harassment on social media. You can't tell them to get counseling. Having access to a classroom or the internet would be a massive luxury, and standing up to their oppressors could get them killed. Counselors are important, but not as important as food and clean water. Their situation is far beyond the confines of this book.

I am completely unqualified to write a book for these girls, since I am coming from a place of great privilege, comparatively. If you're reading this book, you probably are too. It's important to recognize our power and privilege if we're going to be able to help them.

We should absolutely continue to improve our own situations and make progress in our communities. However, it's essential that we remember these girls too. They are just like us, only their lives are in crisis every day. Remember the golden rule of power dynamics from page 25. We have more power than these kids. They have less power than us. They are vulnerable. It's our duty to do what we can to uplift and support them.

Out of all the options on pages 178–183, raising money for established organizations is the best thing you can do for girls who are suffering abroad. Protesting on your own streets won't help them much. You likely won't be able to go to their countries and get involved on a hands-on level until you're much older.

However, if you're interested in raising money for an international sexual abuse cause, reread the section on fund-raising on page 178. Then check out some of these international organizations that would probably take donations.

Child Helpline International, https://www.childhelplineinternational.org/, is a highly ranked global network of 178 toll-free helplines that children can call in a crisis. Callers are connected to a professional who can talk to them and help them get to the next step.

ECPAT (Ending Child Sexual Exploitation), https://www.ecpat.org/, is a global society that takes strong measures to protect children from sex trafficking and exploitation, particularly online and by "sex tourists" who exploit children when visiting foreign countries.

Somewhat similar to Child Helpline, the INHOPE Foundation, http://inhopefoundation.org/, is a network of international hotlines where anyone can report illegal online exploitation, including child pornography.

The International Society for the Prevention of Child Abuse & Neglect (ISPCAN), https://www.ispcan.org/, aims to prevent all forms of child abuse around the world, as well as to educate children and collect important data. Each year ISPCAN hosts a large conference for anti–child abuse organizations from around the world.

UNICEF, https://www.unicef.org/, is an expansive, connected organization that works in 190 countries. The group aids children's health, education, development, and safety around the world. UNICEF has extensive knowledge and resources regarding child sexual abuse victims.

The World Childhood Foundation, https://childhood .org/, supports projects around the world that protect children from sexual abuse and exploitation. The group has spearheaded creative social media movements, including #EyesWideOpen, which asks users to upload a photo of their eyes close-up, a message to abusers that everyone is watching.

Many other organizations combat sex abuse around the world. However, if you search beyond the above list, make sure that you're donating to a nongovernmental organization, or NGO. That's the safest and most official bet.

If you want to start an organization to help raise funds, it will take a lot of research, time, and ambition. But if you have those things, the sky is the limit.

THE LAST STORIES

The following three stories are true.

When Canadian Craig Kielburger was just twelve years old, he was flipping through a newspaper when he found a devastating story. A twelve-year-old child slave from Pakistan had been murdered after standing up for human rights. Inspired and upset, Craig, his older brother, and a few of his fellow seventh graders launched WE Charity. The organization helps families around the globe get on their feet and live sustainably.

When Los Angeles ten-year-old Lulu Cerone heard that a one-dollar glass of lemonade could provide clean drinking water to an African family for a whole year, she was inspired. Eight years later, she has raised $150,000 for clean water and other causes in Africa. Her group LemonAID Warriors provides guidance on how to make activism a part of this generation's social life.

When Neha Gupta was only nine years old, she visited her parents' native home in India. She met orphans who lived in the area and was appalled by their living conditions. She went home to Pennsylvania, sold all her toys, and spent the money to help orphans in one Indian orphanage. Now she runs Empower Orphans, a global charity that has raised over $1.3 million to help impoverished orphans around the globe. Neha won the International Children's Peace Prize in 2014.

CONCLUSION

These are extraordinary stories. It's rare that *anyone* can accomplish such incredible things, let alone a nine-year-old, a ten-year-old, and a twelve-year-old. These kids are amazing, yes, but remember, they also worked very hard. Neha, Lulu, and Craig started small and then put in a super-human amount of dedication and effort. They found their callings, and they went for it.

We need dedicated fighters like these against sexual abuse. We need people to carry the #MeToo flag into their schools, their families, their future jobs, their colleges, and to the voting booths. It will take work, creativity, unity, dedication, empathy, grit, and courage. It will take sex abuse education—as you've learned in this book, there is a *lot* to learn—so you're already ahead of the curve. It will take changes in our laws, our processes, and our ways of thinking. It will take brave allies and even braver victims.

Your journey can start small, just as Craig's, Lulu's, and Neha's journeys did. It can start by speaking up to a friend who uses victim-blaming language or by sharing important information in this book with your friends. Perhaps one day you'll report an abuser (which is a huge undertaking, as you've read), or stand beside a victim as their ally. Maybe you'll start a movement in your school, in your community, or around the globe.

Perhaps most important though, you'll remember that victims of abuse deserve to be protected, empowered, and believed.

You were not born into a perfect or a fair world. We have a very long way to go to eradicate sexual abuse. But don't lose hope. Take Neha's, Lulu's, and Craig's stories, as well as all the stories in this book, and use them as fuel to make the world better. You have more power than you think.

Use it.

ADDITIONAL RESOURCES

All of these organizations played a huge role in this book. This section is a handy guide to sex abuse resources, whether you're a victim or an ally. Continue the fight armed with knowledge and support!

Me Too Movement
https://metoomvmt.org/
While one website couldn't possibly contain the giant that the movement has become, it's a very useful database for anyone looking to get involved or looking for help.

Educational Material

Centers for Disease Control and Prevention
https://www.cdc.gov/violenceprevention/childabuseandneglect
This national government site offers important facts about a wide variety of health topics, including sexual violence and child abuse. The child abuse page offers tips on building a nurturing environment for a child, as well as surveys, fast facts and statistics, and more.

The Dru Sjodin National Sex Offender Public Website
https://www.nsopw.gov/
This government website is run by the US Department of Justice. It contains educational resources as well as the most comprehensive national sex offender registry in the country.

NetSmartz Workshop
https://www.missingkids.org/NetSmartz
This interactive educational program is part of the National Center for Missing & Exploited Children. The program offers lesson plans and activities for kids aged five through seventeen. Through games and presentations, NetSmartz entertains kids while teaching them how to be safe on the internet.

Power Up, Speak Out!
https://powerupspeakout.org/
This fantastic education organization is based in Montana. This book's entire chapter on healthy relationships is based on their teachings. Tell your teachers about it. The group will send your school a fun activity package that will bring their lessons to life.

National Crisis Hotlines and Other Support

These hotlines offer 24-7 support for victims and allies. All calls are confidential.

Childhelp National Child Abuse Hotline
 (800) 4-A-CHILD, or (800) 422-4453
 This hotline serves the United States and Canada in 170 languages. Callers can receive information, referrals, intervention, and more.

Darkness to Light Helpline
 (866) FOR-LIGHT, (866) 367-5444, or the crisis text line, Text "LIGHT" to 741741
 Darkness to Light offers guidance for people in the US who are looking for resources in their local communities.

Forge
 https://forge-forward.org/
 This nonprofit is dedicated to helping trans and gender nonconforming sexual assault survivors. They provide resources and local referrals to counselors.

GLBT National Help Center's LGBT National Youth Talkline
 (800) 246-PRIDE, (800) 246-7743, or online chat at https://www .glbthotline.org/chat.html
 The group provides support for lesbian, gay, bisexual, and transgender youth who are facing difficult issues.

MaleSurvivor
 https://malesurvivor.org/
 This is an online community of male sex abuse survivors.

National Sexual Assault Hotline
 (800) 656-HOPE, or (800) 656-4673
 The hotline is associated with the Rape, Abuse & Incest National Network (RAINN). Trained staff provides support, and you will be routed to local help in your area.

1in6
 https://1in6.org/
 This national helpline is for men and boys who have experienced sexual abuse.

Victim Connect Resource Center
 (855) 4-VICTIM, or (855) 484-2846, or through an online chat at https://chat.victimsofcrime.org/victim-connect/
 This is a confidential place to receive referrals if you are the victim of a crime.

Reporting Hotlines

These hotlines can be used to report sex abuse crimes, including child pornography and abuse:

INHOPE Foundation
   http://www.inhopefoundation.org/
   This website will link you to hotlines in countries across the globe.

The National Center for Missing and Exploited Children CyberTipline
   (800) THE-LOST, or (800) 843-5678
   The hotlines listed above are international or national. Find phone numbers for your state's child services programs at childwelfare. gov/organizations.

National Legal Services
   American Association of University Women (AAUW)
   (800) 326-AAUW, (800) 326-2289, or https://www.aauw.org
   The AAUW promotes equity for all women and girls, lifelong education, and positive societal change.

Child Protective Services

Each state has its own child protective services agency. You can find yours by searching online for your state plus "child protective services." Make sure the website ends in .gov.
This legal resource can help you learn about your state's response system. But to report abuse, call 911 first.

Legal Momentum
   (212) 925-6635 or https://www.legalmomentum.org/
   Legal Momentum works to enforce girls' equal access to education. Their work in this area focuses on how sexual harassment in schools operates as a barrier to equal education.

National Center for Lesbian Rights (NCLR)
   http://www.nclrights.org/
   (800) 528-6257 or (415) 392-6257
   It serves the entire LGBTQ community through advocacy and legal advice.

National Women's Law Center
   (202) 588-5180 or https://nwlc.org/
   The National Women's Law Center works to protect and advance the progress of women and girls at work, in school, and in virtually every aspect of their lives.

Office of Civil Rights

> https://wdcrobcolp01.ed.gov/CFAPPS/OCR/contactus.cfm
> Visit this site to find the contact information for your local office of civil rights.

US Department of Education: Office of Civil Rights

> (800) 421-3481
> https://www2.ed.gov/ocr
> This federal agency enforces school sexual harassment laws. You can call the hotline to report any educational discrimination and to request information on filing discrimination complaints.

Nonprofit Resources

In chapter 6, I talked about nonprofits that are specifically against childhood sexual abuse. However, many more nonprofits throughout the United States handle broader issues in addition to sexual abuse, including child physical abuse and the abuse of women. The following are just a few:

Childhelp

> https://www.childhelp.org/
> Childhelp offers child abuse prevention programs, intervention programs, and treatment programs for child victims across the country.

Child Welfare Information Gateway

> https://www.childwelfare.gov/organizations/
> This website, part of the US Department of Health and Human Services, has a lot of handy lists, including national and state nonprofits, as well as government agencies that fight child abuse.

Internal Revenue Service

> https://www.irs.gov/charities-and-nonprofits
> You can search the IRS website to make sure that a national nonprofit is legitimate. This does not apply to organizations based outside of the United States.

Joyful Heart Foundation

> http://www.joyfulheartfoundation.org/
> Founded by actor Mariska Hargitay, Joyful Heart Foundation offers healing, advocacy, and education services to fight all sexual assault, child abuse, and domestic violence.

The Kempe Center

> http://www.kempe.org/

Founded by a doctor, the Kempe Center offers treatment to victims of child abuse, as well as child welfare training and research. Kempe also raises money in the field of child abuse.

National Center for Victims of Crime
https://victimsofcrime.org/
To benefit victims of all crimes including abuse, this organization offers extensive educational resources, legal information, national conferences, and more.

Fundraising

Information about fundraising can be found on page 178. Here are some further resources:

Grants—Children's Bureau, of the Administration for Children and Families
https://www.acf.hhs.gov/cb/grants
This site offers national grants for programs that combat sexual abuse against children.

McGinnes, Lisa. *The Young Adult's Guide to School Fundraising 101.* Ocala, FL: Atlantic, 2017.

Office of Sex Offender Sentencing, Monitoring, Apprehending, Registering and Tracking (SMART)
https://www.smart.gov/
This government agency is a great resource for national legal information, and it also provides grant money through its website.

Statistics and Resources on Child Sexual Abuse

Children's Bureau: An Office of the Administration for Children and Families
https://www.acf.hhs.gov/cb
If you're looking for national statistics in the United States, this is a great resource. The Children's Bureau collects extensive data in its annual Child Maltreatment report.

Out of the Shadows
https://outoftheshadows.eiu.com/
This huge and extremely important study, released in 2019, covers 70 percent of the world's children in forty countries. The study measured and ranked each country's reaction toward children's sexual abuse.

UNICEF
https://www.unicef.org/
UNICEF is a massive organization that tracks trends in sexual violence around the world, as well as other forms of violence, health issues, education, and more. You can search for data by country as well as globally.

Memoirs

Angelou, Maya. *I Know Why the Caged Bird Sings*. New York: Random House, 2002.
This classic, heartbreaking book, originally published in 1969, details Angelou's childhood sexual abuse beginning at the age of eight, as well as the racial oppression she faced in the 1930s.

Book, Lauren. *It's Okay to Tell: A Story of Hope and Recovery*. Westport, NY: Easton Studio, 2011.
The true story of a girl who was abused by her female nanny for years, right under her family's nose.

Healing

Lohmann, Raychelle Cassada, and Sheela Raja. *The Sexual Trauma Workbook for Teen Girls: A Guide to Recovery from Sexual Assault and Abuse*. Oakland: Instant Help Books, 2016.
An empowering step-by-step book about healing, written by a doctor and a social worker.

Mather, Cynthia L. *How Long Does It Hurt? A Guide to Recovering from Physical and Sexual Abuse for Teenagers, Their Friends, and Their Families*. San Francisco: Jossey-Bass, 2014.
Survivor of incest Cynthia Mather provides a step-by-step guide for teenagers who are healing from sexual trauma.

Gartner, Richard B., ed. *Healing Sexually Betrayed Men and Boys: Treatment for Sexual Abuse, Assault, and Trauma*. New York: Routledge, 2017.
Experts contributed to this resource for men and boys who are healing from sexual abuse trauma.

INDEX

ACKNOWLEDGMENTS

Power Up, Speak Out!; Kelsi Helsey; Libby Johnson; Darkness to Light; Gwen Bouchie; Steve Mandell; Stop Sexual Assault in Schools; Dr. Esther Warkov; Dr. Joel Levin; Dr. Cheryl Graf; Carrie Goldberg, Esq.; Stop It Now; my amazing therapist Allison; our friends, parents, all the caregivers who helped carry the production of this book, and all the amazing people who shared their personal stories.

ABOUT THE CONTRIBUTORS

Halley Bondy is a professional freelance writer, journalist, editor, producer, and mom based in Brooklyn. You can find her articles in NBC News, Daily Beast, DAME Magazine, Eater NY, Bustle, Romper, The Outline, Oxygen, CMT, Scary Mommy, Vice, *New York Daily News*, MTV, and more. She writes scripts for the "Masters of Scale" podcast, and she's written for "You Must Remember This."

Halley has written three books. Most recently, she published *Speak Up!*, a how-to for middle school girls on finding their confidence. Her other books include a babysitting how-to called *Don't Sit on the Baby* and *77 Things You Absolutely Have to Do Before You Graduate College*.

Halley's work has won a Shorty Award for digital content, as well as the Outstanding Playwright award at the Fringe NYC Festival. NBC gave her a GEM award, which stands for "Going the Extra Mile." She lives in Brooklyn with her husband and daughter.

Timothy Corbett is an artist, designer, and manufacturing specialist. His work includes delicate ink and gouache drawings, a line of fine hand tools for woodworkers, and large-scale collaborative sculptures and installations. These have appeared in galleries and performances throughout New York, and in Red Hook, Brooklyn, where he maintains a personal studio.

Currently, Tim is helping to build a fleet of six-foot tall museums with a team that believes in equal access to fundamental knowledge. He is a proud alum of the School of Art at the Cooper Union for the Advancement of Science and Art, and the A.W. Dreyfoos School of the Arts.

He lives in Brooklyn with his wife, Halley, and his daughter, Robin.